We Can Still Cw...

by

Phil Doherty

Chapter One

Welcome/Croeso

The top half of the sign that greeted drivers on their way into the village of Aberglas read, "Os Gallwch Ddarellen Croeso Hon" which translates as: "If you can read this, 'Welcome'". The bottom half of the sign - written in English - read: "If not, bugger off. We're not a tourist town".

This was not the original sign put up by the council. That was taken down by the villagers a while back. But if you did "Siarad Cymraeg" [speak Welsh] or were brave or stupid enough to enter without being able to speak the language then after a quarter of a mile you would reach Upper High Street with its selection of shops either side. One of these was a woollen business run by Gwyneth Owens - always known by her full name - as another Gwyneth ran the café.

The locals decided to call both Gwyneths by their full names in order to avoid confusion. This made perfect sense to them but would baffle the hell out of any visitor as Gwyneth Owens was a petite size eight whilst Gwyneth Thomas, the café owner, was a hefty size twenty - attributable to her personal sampling of all new recipes before serving them up to the public.

These ladies were the only two residents of Upper High Street not named after their occupation. The Post Office was run by 'Paula the Post'; the Newsagents by husband and wife Daffydd and Mair Jones - or 'Mair and Daffydd paper shop'. If you turned left at the end of Upper High Street you entered Lower High Street and two miles later would end up on the road to Brynlog, taking you out of the village. Yet if you turned right instead, 50 yards up on the left opposite the village green was the *Dragon and Daffodil* public house - run by 'Megan and Dai the Pub'.

Now the main reason for the change of the welcome sign was what had happened two years previously: it was the middle of August, a typical summer's day in Wales with heavy rain and fog. All of a sudden a coach pulled up outside Dai's pub. On board were 55 American tourists on a ten-day tour of the castles of England and Wales.

They had been on their way to Llancoch Castle but as a result of the weather, had been informed by a phone call from the ticket office there that their journey could be delayed by up to three hours. Llancoch's representative asked the tour guide for their location and upon learning that they were near the village of Aberglas informed them that they would get a very warm welcome at the *Dragon and Daffodil* Public House. They were only 45 minutes from the castle so would have time for a meal and a drink. The alternative was a three-hour wait on the bus outside Llancoch Castle. Twenty-one minutes later the bus pulled up outside the *Dragon and Daffodil*.

The door opened and the travel guide, an Englishman, entered the pub. He asked Dai if he served pub lunches and if so could he also cope with 55 extra people all at once? Dai stuck out his chest.

"Of course mun [man] but it's the chef's day off and I am unable to contact her."

What he should have said was Megan, his wife, had gone to Brynlog to meet her sister for a game of bingo and that he was not going to disturb her out of fear for his life. Dai instead announced that 'today's menu would be minimal'. The guide accepted Dai's explanation and returned to the bus. After a brief consultation with his passengers, a show of hands quickly voted in favour of the meal there.

First to the bar was a big, brash middle-aged American wearing a 'Hey I'm Chuck' badge and 'Born in the USA' baseball cap.

"Hey buddy" he said to Dai, looking around the pub then back at his fellow companions before staring once more at Dai. "What's with all the weird words on your walls?" pointing to some 'Cymru Am Byth' [Wales forever] and 'Croeso I'r Rdraig A Daff' [Welcome to the Dragon and Daff]. "And also I noticed the weird words on your signpost when we entered your quaint little village…"

Dai could feel his blood starting to boil. Yet he held back, explaining that it was Welsh, his mother's tongue, and a language that went back generations before her. The

American looked at him in disbelief and confusion. Then once again, in a voice loud enough for everyone in the bar to hear, asked:

"Dai, why have your own language when your quaint little Wales is part of the same old little country of England?"

Once again Dai bit his tongue but inside he was outraged. Normally they would have been evicted from his premises quicker than a bat out of hell but the money they were paying there stopped him. Further, what he had planned for Chuck and his group that afternoon meant that Dai would have the last laugh.

The guide could see that Dai was getting more than a little annoyed. He therefore walked over to the bar and cleared his throat loudly. He asked Dai what choice of meals, given the circumstances, were available? Dai looked at the guide, smiled and explained that they only had a choice of one meal. Knowing how much the Americans loved the Royal Family Dai explained that any new Prince of Wales could only become a Prince after stopping at his pub and eating the traditional Welsh dish to prove his worthiness and commitment to his beloved country.

The American, who by now had assumed the role of group-mouthpiece, turned round to repeat to his fellow travel companions that the meal on offer was by Royal Appointment. When asked if they were all happy at the prospect of a royal banquet being served, everyone nodded vehemently. Dai smiled as the group swallowed that tale; what they would actually be served would not be swallowed so well.

Dai went to the kitchen and took a deep breath. He picked up the phone to dial the *Brynlog Inn* knowing his wife and sister-in-law always had a meal and a drink there before bingo. David, the landlord, was a very old friend of his as they had worked down the mines together and had both entered the pub trade after their closures.

The phone rang twice. A familiar voice answered:
"*Brynlog Inn*, Dai speaking."
"Hi Dai, it's Dai the Pub."
"Hello Dai," said Dai the Inn.
"How's business butte [friend]?"

"How's it going, busy is you?" Dai asked.

"Got 55 Americans in here and I need to speak to 'She who must be obeyed', replied Dai the Pub.

"You sure you want to do that, butte? I have been your friend for many a year and this sounds like a suicide mission. You do know she's here with your sister-in-law Blodwyn, don't you?"

"I know but I'm desperate. Do you think I would be that tup [thick] to phone her otherwise?"

"Well," Dai said. "I will give her a shout. Good luck butte: it's been nice knowing you,"

Dai then heard Dai the Inn shout to Megan:

"Dai's on the phone, love. He needs to speak to you urgent like."

Dai could hear Megan heading towards the phone saying to Blodwyn that 'he better be phoning me to tell me he's dead otherwise, when I get hold of him, he will wish he was'. Dai screwed up his eyes.

"David Davies. This had better be a matter of life or death - or something more serious."

"Listen love," braved Dai. "You know that new washing machine you wanted off the catalogue 80 weeks at £4.27 a week? Well, if you get back here with what I need, I will take you back to Brynlog tomorrow and buy it for you in cash."

"Dai love…"

Dai knew by that reply that she had calmed down.

"But Dai love…the catalogue people are not here in Brynlog. They are in England, love."

Dai shook his head and raised his eyes - but then stopped in case she knew he was doing it.

"No, we can buy one with cash tomorrow - not on the weekly. Now please love: I only need two things."

"Well, can't you wait love? In the bingo this afternoon, if I call a house on the pink flyer on an odd number in under 30 numbers, I will win an extra £50."

"Megan love," Dai nearly started shouting at her but taking a deep breath continued, "I got 50 Americans in here and I am going to charge them £5 each for Cocos and Bara

Lawr" [cockles and lava bread: a very popular welsh dish of edible seaweed, distinct in taste and blackness].

"Well! Why didn't you say earlier? I will be there in 20 minutes. Blodwyn's not drinking today, due to the tablets. The Doctor said she had to finish the course before she could drink again. It's her bits and bobs playing up again."

Dai cringed then interrupted once again.

"Megan love, tell me later. I need you and the food here now - and please hurry! My clean shirts depend on it"

With that the phone went dead and Dai returned to the bar to continue serving until Megan arrived.

Thirty minutes later, the kitchen door opened and in rushed Megan with five carrier bags full of cockles and lava bread. Within 20 minutes the first four people to be served looked on in disbelief and horror at what was on their plates.

Even though it was over two years ago, Dai still regaled his regulars with the story of the day the Americans who had invaded his pub arrived looking nice and suntanned but left with faces greener than the mountains overlooking his pub and the village green in front of it. Although he never had many tourists visit, Dai still made a tidy living from the locals - apart from Sundays when the pub would open but could not serve alcohol as it was against the law of the chapel. It soon became the only dry village left in Wales.

Dai tried different ideas to boost his business. One month he advertised a quiz. To make it fair he had all the names taken out of a hat, ending up with six teams of four. It was going really well until the answers for the second round on Local History were announced. Then everyone started arguing with Dai, saying that his answers were wrong. 'Dragon's Breath''s team captain declared that his Grandfather was there at the time of the question and then someone from 'Daffs Delight''s team asserted that the captain of 'Dragon's Breath' was also wrong because his Grandmother was there and had not seen his Grandfather.

That was the first and last time a pub quiz was held. Two months later Dai had another brainwave: he decided to hire a karaoke machine, complete with professional compere. Dai had seen the advertisement in the *Brynlog Bugle*. The pub was duly packed out. Indeed seven days beforehand everyone in the village had been walking around singing in readiness for their big night.

All the men from the choir turned up in their official uniform of white trousers, violet shirts, purple dickie bows and black blazers bearing their embroidered crest of a dragon on top of a castle. The compere emerged from the lounge and grabbed his microphone with a "Good evening the *Dragon and Daff*. Are you ready to rock this joint?" He then started singing a heavy rock number and by the time he had finished ten people had got up and left, complaining that if that was the only song he had, it was too loud and a waste of money.

Then, after an hour of six 'Calon Lans' and eight versions of Tom Jones' 'Delilah' the compere pulled the plug out of the machine and handed Dai his money back. He then grabbed his mic, promising to return in the morning for the machine. With that he got in his car and sped off.

Another of Dai's bright ideas was to hold the meeting for the Bryncoch branch of Alcoholics Anonymous in the lounge as it had a separate entrance from the bar and was only ever hired out for private functions. With its crushed velvet carpet it had enough seats and tables to accommodate over 60 people. It had a different bar behind which he would personally serve, making Megan work from the public bar, and he promised his customers that he would not disclose their identity: their secret would be safe with him. Dai had even taken photographs of the lounge and sent them to the Bryncoch Alcoholics Anonymous branch, together with £10. In the letter he also explained that the lounge bar was only ever used for funeral wakes so that there would be no problem booking it for as long as they wanted - as long as no-one died. It would be available from six until eleven any week night. Yet despite his offer, the following week the Chairman of the branch replied with the following:

Alcoholics Anonymous
Bryncoch Branch
25 Upper Lower New Street
Bryncoch

Dear Mr Dai the Pub Thomas

I would like to take this opportunity to thank you for your invitation to hold our meetings at your establishment.

The price you quoted for the hire of your lounge bar was very favourable and also the offer of soup and bread in a basket for £3.50 per member was also considered.

The second offer also of a reduction in price of selected house doubles at a price of £2.50 was also taken into consideration.

But unfortunately after careful consideration by the committee, we have decided to decline your kind offer but would like to take this opportunity to thank you once again.

Kindest regards

Cyril Owens

Dai looked at the letter, crumpled it up and chucked it in the bin. Out loud he said to himself that he should have offered cockles and lava bread instead of soup and bread. Then again, it is most probably too far to travel every week, he thought. So, he went to the kitchen and put the kettle on.

Then, two years back, one of the big internet service providers contacted Brynlog Council offering to install underground cables for Aberglas. This would enable them all to have access to the World Wide Web.

An emergency village meeting was called and a week later, in a packed Welfare Hall, the Chairman of Brynlog Council with two representatives from the Internet Company delivered their proposal. After just over an hour the villagers rejected it.

The first objection was that Bryn the Post had once mistakenly delivered mail to Number 22 instead of 23 and he knew them, so how could some computer who does not know them be able to find the right address to send them an e-mail?

The second objection was that Dai the Pub had once read in the paper that a massive computer virus had hit over two million homes. He duly reminded the villagers of the outbreak, a few centuries ago, of a plague that had killed many people and also an epidemic of foot-and-mouth that had nearly wiped out the farmers' livelihood 75 years later.

Dai the Pub had also phoned the chemist in Brynlog to ask if they had any tablets to stop them getting a computer virus? He was informed that no such tablets were available.

Despite the safety explanations from the internet representatives it was decided to reject the installation as it would be safer for all of the village and the livestock.

However, the villagers still had access to satellite television if they wished. Yet most of them had decided instead to use the Freeview box given to them by Brynlog Council at the point of digital changeover as the majority only ever watched the main four channels.

The villagers' main objection to a satellite dish was their pre-payment of the television licence fee: they were not going to be paying any extra.

The village of Aberglas itself was surrounded by beautiful mountains and countryside but this did cause a problem for anyone wishing to use a mobile phone here. The only way you could get a signal was to clamber 100 feet up the mountain. Only then would you be successful - which meant that only the youngsters of the village used mobiles as they were the only ones who could climb up the mountain.

One of the oldest residents, Mrs Jones, had her home telephone removed a long time ago. Her reason was that during the first week of installation she had received two telephone calls. The first call informed her that her Aunt had died and the following day a second call told her that a friend had also passed away. She therefore had it removed because it only gave her bad news.

Despite Mrs Jones being one of the oldest residents in the village, the self-proclaimed 'Voice of the Village' as well as being Chairperson of the local parish council, was Mrs Morgan Morgan.

Mrs Morgan Morgan had been a hospital matron for over 40 years but had now retired. Over that time she had seen some radical changes in the Health Service but always insisted that when she was in charge, the hospitals were run properly.

She often told people that the trouble with today's hospitals was that the patients could have visitors day and night and also watch television. Instead they should remember they were there to get better as it's a hospital - not a holiday camp.

Mrs Morgan Morgan further maintained that when she was in charge the nurses did not have a comfy office in which to relax. Instead there would be a desk at one end of the ward from where they would work and keep an eye on all the patients. If someone had a bad chest or cough they were encouraged to smoke a cigarette as it would clear their lungs.

When Mrs Morgan Morgan retired a rumour circulated that all the hospital staff, including most of the patients, had contributed towards a collection and bought her a one-way plane ticket to Australia – a claim vehemently denied by Mrs Morgan Morgan to anyone who was brave or stupid enough to ask her.

Mrs Morgan Morgan had been married three times. Her first husband, Mr Jones, had died in his sleep; her second husband, Mr Thomas, had died of a heart attack whilst gardening, and her last husband, Mr Morgan, had also passed away in his sleep.

When she was asked why she was called Mrs Morgan Morgan she explained that the Morgan family to whom she belonged had been part of Welsh history for centuries, so she had refused to change her name. Mrs Morgan Morgan explained that at birth she was Miss Morgan. When she married her first husband she became Mrs Morgan

Jones. After she married Mr Thomas, she was Mrs Morgan Thomas; and when she married for the final time she became Mrs Morgan Morgan.

She never remarried after her third husband had passed away. When Mr Morgan died, a rumour started that the husbands chose to die just for the peace and quiet. There was also another rumour circulating that the Co-op Funeral Services had offered her a loyalty card and her own car parking space there.

Every morning at 8.45 she would leave her house to walk to the local shop for her morning paper. She always dressed in black including a black umbrella and black hat with a black flower on it. Even the Co-op undertakers were more colourful than her.

The Deputy Chairperson of the Parish Council was the Reverend Ivor Emmanuel. He had been the Reverend of Aberglas for over 20 years and had married and buried a lot of the villagers in that time. He was also famous for his diverse sermons ranging from the uplifting - leaving the congregation with joy in their hearts and the promise of internal happiness in the Kingdom of Heaven - to the blood-and-thunder addresses, where everyone was going to scream for eternity in the fiery pits of Hell.

The chapel itself had been built originally in the 16th Century and had not changed much. As you passed through the wrought iron gates they groaned and squeaked. Heading up the path towards the chapel you would witness the most recent graves but if you detoured to the back of the building you would be confronted by the original graveyard.

These graves dated back to the chapel origins, most being surrounded by large iron railings placed to protect them from both wild animals and grave robbers.

The most famous occupant buried there was the so-called 'Witch of Bledwyn'. The story was that in the late 16th Century a middle-aged woman who lived nearby was accused of witchcraft after she was seen drinking and dancing on a Sunday. As it was against church rules she was deemed to be a witch. She was therefore burnt at the stake, her ashes being covered in holy water and buried on hallowed ground. The church believed that no witch could enter hallowed ground so they would be able to raise her from the dead.

The Bledwyn witch had been tried and convicted simply for drinking on a Sunday. Five hundred years later and you still could not drink on a Sunday in Aberglas…

Aberglas was ten miles from the main town of Brynlog. The villagers could get the once-a-week bus service to do their big shop there. If the locals ran out of anything beforehand there was the local grocery shop in the village, run by 'Sian the Shop' . You could buy milk and bread there in additional to other small sundries. Next door was the post office run by 'Paula the Post'. It sold stationery and stamps as the village had refused the internet installation, obliging them to continue to write to each other as they had for hundreds of years.

The Treasurer of the Parish Council was Police Constable David Williams. He had been with the force for over 40 years, serving with the London Metropolitan for 30 years before accepting the Aberglas post. He was offered the post because he was born and bred in Aberton, some 50 miles away but was classed as a local due to the fact that he was Welsh.

P.C. Williams occupied a house with a cellar that you could lock so that it could also be used as a cell until the prisoner could be transferred to Brynlog police station. Unlike other police cells, however, this one had a television, a three-piece suite, a bed, a toilet and a couple of nice lamps.

During P.C. Williams' ten years here he had only had to use the cellar as a cell once. It occurred when one of the villagers, 'Morgan the Brewer', had got drunk and forgot where he lived. Despite P.C. Williams knowing where he lived, he thought it would be safer for him to stay there that night because if he had taken Morgan home, Morgan's wife would have killed him - and that involved too much paperwork.

Chapter Two

The Letter

It was just past 8.30 on a Monday morning when Bryn the Post knocked on the Reverend Emmanuel's door.

The door opened and there as always, dressed in his full outfit, stood the Reverend with a mug in his hand and a strong smell of coffee wafting from it. On the mug was written 'Don't cross me till I've finished my coffee'.

"Hello Reverend Emmanuel," Bryn beamed. "I have this letter for you."

The Reverend took it from Bryn's hand.

"Have you seen this?" asked the Reverend, pointing at the letter box. "It would have fitted in there, so there was no need to disturb me from my morning coffee, was there?"

"I know," retorted Bryn "but this looks important. It's from the Mayor's office of Brynlog himself."

The Reverend turned the envelope over and looked at the return address. It was indeed from the Mayor's office. He passed his coffee mug over to Bryn and opened it. Taking out his glasses from his inside pocket he started to read it to himself. Then he looked at Bryn.

"This is an outrage. I need you to knock on every door on your round and tell them that there will be an urgent meeting at the Welfare Hall tonight at 7pm and it's in the best interest of all to attend. Now, go quickly."

Bryn nodded. "Yes Reverend" and quickly headed down the path. Nearing the gate, the Reverend called him back. As Bryn approached the Reverend opened his hand. Bryn went to shake it but then realised that the Reverend had only wanted his coffee back. Bryn had been in such a rush that he had taken the Reverend's coffee with him.

"If you wanted a coffee that desperately, you should have said. I wouldn't have minded making you one and it would have saved you taking mine. Now, do you want to come in for a coffee?"

"Yes thank you Reverend. I would love to," smiled Bryn about to enter.

Well, you're out of luck boyo. You haven't got time. You are on a mission for God - well, myself actually but I'm on very good terms with him. So now get going and make sure everyone knows about the meeting tonight!"

At 7pm the Reverend Ivor Emmanuel rose from his chair and cleared his throat. The room fell silent. On his left sat Mrs Morgan Morgan; to his right, P.C. Williams.

"Evening ladies and gentleman," greeted the Reverend. "I would have preceded this welcome with the word 'Good' but after receiving this letter from Brynlog Mayor's office this morning, there is nothing 'good' about it. Now, I don't want any shouting or outbursts as I read this to you: there will be plenty of time for that later."

Dai the Pub raised his hand and waited for the Reverend to acknowledge him. Mrs Morgan Morgan observed it first and told 'David the Public House' to wait until he had finished.

Mrs Morgan Morgan would never shorten anyone's names. She always insisted that "it's a lazy person who couldn't be bothered to pronunciate the full word".

Mrs Morgan Morgan had once written to Yorkshire Television Studios to complain after watching her first episode of *Emmerdale Farm* that one of the main actors had told his wife he was going to "top field". The writers had clearly misspelled the actor's line as it should have read that he was "going up to the top field" instead. Also, could they ask the actors not to use such a silly accent?

Mrs Morgan Morgan also stated in her letter that you would never find any programme filmed in Wales consisting of only the Welsh language. After three days without a reply she decided never to watch another episode again. Today she would only ever watch one soap: *Pobol-y-Cwm*, on S4C.

The Reverend Emmanuel took out his glasses from his inside pocket and cleared his throat once again.

"To the Chairperson of Aberglas Parish Council,

It has come to our attention that Aberglas has somehow not been allocated or twinned with any other

European city. This oversight we believe is partly our fault and partly yours so we must remedy this as soon as possible."

The crowd started to murmur and shout "No way this is happening". Once again the Reverend raised his hand.
"I told you to wait until I have finished."
The crowd quietened and he resumed out loud:

"Therefore after an extensive search we have found a village that is not twinned with anyone either so we have decided to proceed with twinning Aberglas with the village of Banka in Hungary.

We will send you more details once we have organised the date for the twinning ceremony.

We hope you will be as excited at the prospect of the twinning as much as we are. We also believe that it will be a financial boost to your village as no doubt after you have become twin towns with Banka you will see an influx of tourists from your sister village.

We will also organise a new village signpost for you, stating your achievement. This will be made at no cost to yourselves and will replace the official signpost which is currently at the entrance of your village.

We are sure you will welcome this exciting prospect and look forward to hearing from you in the near future.

Yours sincerely

George Thomas

(Mayor's office, Brynlog)

The Reverend Emmanuel removed his glasses and stated that the floor was now open. However, you would only be acknowledged if you raised your hand first. Mrs Morgan Morgan stood up declaring that she was not standing for this and promptly sat down again.
Reverend Emmanuel then noticed Dai the Pub's raised hand.

"Yes, David?"
Dai got to his feet.
"Well, I for one would welcome any tourists to the *Dragon and Daffodil* as long as they are not American and can speak Welsh."
The assembly burst out laughing. Undeterred, Dai continued,
"If this actually happens with this place in Hungary, does it mean I have to put Hungarian goulash on the menu? I mean, the only stew we do is cawl [welsh lamb or beef soup] and that's not even a stew, it's a soup. I mean, I'm confused already and that's before we even have to learn the Hungarian language."
He then sat down. P.C. Williams now raised his arm and upon acknowledgement stood up to enquire whether twinning this village in Hungary would mean obligatory entry into the Euro, like the rest of Europe?
"At the moment I know as well as most of you do, that some countries are in financial difficulties so bad that if they tried to get a loan it would take them at least a thousand years to pay it back."
The crowd immediately started clapping in agreement. P.C. Williams stated that he had taken out a loan from a Building Society many years ago to buy a car and that it took him five years to repay it. The car had apparently broken down after three years so he was paying two more years for nothing. He concluded with the announcement:
"Also in Wales, when we are going to the toilet we say we are going to spend a penny. But if we have to change currencies does that mean we will have to 'euro-nate' instead?"
Once again the crowd burst into laughter but the mood quickly became more serious. Reverend Emmanuel stood up again and reminded everyone what had happened ten years ago when they had applied to Brynlog Council for a grant to erect a war memorial for local World War Two victim, Gyynfor Davies.
Mr Davies had died in 1942 but was not on active service nor caught in an air raid. Luckily, Aberglas was never bombed and had even taken a couple of refugees from the

bigger towns, returning them after the war. Just dying during the war was enough for the locals to want to commemorate him on the village green, which now bears his name.

Actually what really happened to poor Gwynfor Davies was that he had just finished his shift down the mine at six o'clock in the evening and had started to make his way home. He decided to stop off at the *Dragon and Daffodil* for a well-deserved pint of mild but one drink led to another. He left the pub about three hours later, slightly worse for wear.

It was winter and therefore dark by four o'clock in the afternoon. There was also a blackout as bombing raids hit London. Gwynfor started to stumble home. This entailed crossing a little river. It was only about six feet wide and a foot deep. There was a bridge further up but Gwynfor had decided that it really was a bridge too far. He therefore resolved that it would be quicker just to cross the water. At any rate it would clean the coal and soot from his boots.

He waded half-way across when the amount of alcohol he had consumed, combined with the temperature of the water, forced him to stop and relieve himself. He then turned to carry on home but suddenly slipped and banged his head on a rock, knocking himself unconscious. He therefore drowned.

Despite the decades of letters sent to Brynlog Council since, their collective plea had been refused every time. The Reverend shook his head at the sad tale.

"And now they want us to be twinned with a foreign town?! Well, before we let this happen the Devil will be wearing ice skates to work!"

This prompted massive applause: if Brynlog Council thought this twinning was going to be easy, they would be in for the shock of their lives.

Mrs Morgan Morgan stood up once more, seeking sensible ideas as to how to block this process with an unknown town and a non-Welsh speaking country?

Paula the Post raised her hand. Mrs Morgan Morgan acknowledged her. "Yes Paula the Post Office. What is your contribution to this meeting?

Paula stood up and timidly confronted the hall:

"Could we just tell Brynlog County Council that we are already twinned with a different village in a different country so that they leave us alone? You never know, it might work..."

Mrs Morgan Morgan rolled her eyes skywards.

"When I was a matron for 37 years, I always told the nurses that they could ask any question as no question is ever stupid. But just now you proved me wrong with that stupid question."

She glared at Paula who quickly looked away from Mrs Morgan Morgan.

"Now, I repeat: is there anyone here with a sensible, serious idea? Please raise your hand and wait for my acknowledgment."

She scanned the room. No hands went up. It was as if the rest of the villagers were just too scared after Paula's humiliation.

Suddenly, from the back of the hall a brave soul raised her hand. It belonged to Mair the Paper Shop. Mrs Morgan Morgan signalled her to collect her thoughts before speaking.

"Before you say something, please tell me that it's a sensible, serious idea. Otherwise, please sit back down so that you don't waste everyone's - including my - precious time."

Mair stood her ground.

"Actually, I have two ideas in mind. My first is to ask Brynlog Council if we can choose a different place to twin with, perhaps somewhere like Pont-Cochglas? My cousin lives there. It's down on the east coast of Wales and I stayed there a couple of years back when she got married. It's a bit like our village here and they speak Welsh almost as good as us. Also it's only a couple of hours away by car."

Mrs Morgan Morgan smiled at Mair.

"That's actually not a bad idea."

She then turned to P.C. Williams:

"Write that down please, Police Constable Williams. At last we have a sensible, serious proposal. Now, Mair, do you want to quit while your'e ahead or is your second idea as good as your first?"

Mair rose once more from her chair:

"My second suggestion is that we could always all of us write a letter of complaint and take it to Brynlog Council in person. Then they can't say that they have never received any of the letters."

There was a murmur of agreement from the crowd and once again Mrs Morgan Morgan smiled. Without looking at him, she instructed:

"Police Constable Williams: write that one down also"

Mair sat down with a big grin. Turning to Daffydd, she beamed:

"I'm not just a pretty face am I?"

"I never said you had a pretty face," he retorted smiling - and then flinched as she elbowed him straight in the stomach.

Back on stage Mrs Morgan Morgan once again asked for any more ideas,

"...or forever keep your mouth shut."

She scanned the room but no-one spoke.

"In that case, it's now 7.57pm and the meeting is closed."

Mrs Morgan Morgan would never say "It was just gone five to or nearly ten past"; she was always exact with the time. It was just another of her strange quirks people had simply got used to during the years.

"I suggest then that you all go home and start writing out letters of complaint ready for us to present to those Euro councillors of Brynlog."

At this point Dai the Pub stood up exclaiming,

"You do know that they are not actually Euro councillors, as they are only a couple of miles up the road, mun? Anyway, I always find it better to think after a couple of drinks. It sort of lubricates the brain - and if any one agrees with me I will be opening the *Drag and Daff* in about ten minutes as I have already lost business being here for nearly an hour."

Dai smiled knowing that by saying 'nearly an hour' instead of '57 minutes' would wind up Mrs Morgan Morgan. Turning round to grab his coat from the chair, he heard Mrs Morgan Morgan again pipe up, stating that Brynlog was in

Wales and Wales was in Europe. So therefore that did indeed make them Euro councillors.

Pleased to have the last word she sat down and announced that the meeting was officially closed but would whoever was the last person to leave please ensure that they turned off the light and returned the key to Reverend Emmanuel for safe keeping.

Everyone realised they were free to go, with about 80 people deciding to take up Dai's offer and head straight off to the *Drag and Daff* to seek some of his liquid inspiration.

Dai issued them all with free paper and pens. It was strange for him as he was not known for his generosity. Megan even stated that if her husband ever had Double Pneumonia he would be too tight to give one away.

The reason for Dai's generosity was the fact that every sheet of writing paper here bore the pub's location details on it. Everyone therefore who was on Brynlog County Council would know where his pub was after reading all the complaints, and might just decide to hold their Christmas party or any other celebration there in the future. Dai smiled at Megan.

"This is the best and most cost-effective advertising I have ever done. Do you think we should write to the other councils in Wales to let them what's happening here?"

Megan looked at him askance.

"You're only saying that to get more free advertising. Dai, I can read you like a book."

Dai smiled back at her.

"Megan, my love. It was the last thing on my mind. But as you now mention it, I can't see it doing any harm."

Megan shook her head.

"I only have one thing to say to you David the Public House. Don't just stand there. Start writing the letters!"

Dai smiled and gave Megan a big peck on the cheek.

"Yes my love."

Megan wiped the cheek he had just kissed.

"Stop that at once! It's not your birthday for another two months. Don't you start getting all amorous like that and especially in front of the public. Remember, don't make love on the garden gate. Love may be blind but the neighbours ain't."

Megan had remembered that verse written on a Valentine's card many years ago and had used it every time Dai had gone to kiss her or hold her hand in public. She could recall many other sayings, with some actually being good advice while others would simply confuse people. One of Megan's favourite sayings was, 'Don't cry over spilt milk. Get a tissue and clean it up before it stains'. It seemed as if she absorbed a lot of sayings and then jumbled them up to suit herself.

Dai had taken a pen and some paper. He sat on Megan's stool at the end of the bar and was scrawling furiously. Normally Megan would not let anyone sit on her bar stool but today she made an exception. Two years back a stranger had come into the pub asking for directions. He was lost on his way to Llancoch Castle and after one of the locals had assisted, the stranger decided to have a soft drink before continuing his journey – and he chose Megan's bar stool without knowing it, to enjoy the drink. It was his bad luck that Megan had decided to frequent the bar herself for a cup of tea and a chat with some of the regulars. She then stopped in horror upon noticing the stranger on her stool.

"Is that stool comfortable?" she asked him.

"Yes," he smiled, "but it dips a bit in the middle. The cushion must have been well used or sat on by some very fat people!" he laughed.

Five minutes of Megan's abuse ensued which, when she gets annoyed, becomes a tirade half in English and half in Welsh. The stranger must have wished that he was driving a time-machine rather than a Renault. Luckily, he had been given correct directions to the castle before Megan's rant - and her alternative route suggestions. Unsurprisingly, the gentleman was never seen again, nor was Megan's bar stool ever occupied intentionally or by mistake - until this evening, when Dai sat on it.

Dai put his pen down after five minutes and took a big gulp of his pint.

"That was easy!" he exclaimed.

He started looking around the pub, surmising to his wife that,

"These lot must be writing a bestseller, the amount of time they are taking to write their letters."

He then announced that there was a two-drink minimum each for the use of the stationery. Everyone laughed except Dai. He was serious but Megan hushed him down, telling him not to be so mean.

"David you are so tight you would not give a door a slam," she smiled. "OK Shakespeare. Let's hear what words of wisdom you have penned to the other councils."

Dai passed her the first sheet.

"You only need one, love. I have written the same on all of the letters."

Megan read what Dai had written. Just under the pub logo were the words: 'Open six days a week: eleven until eleven. Bar meals available between twelve and eight; beer garden at the back. Phone for further details'.

Megan stared at Dai and then back at the paper.

"Are you seriously going to send them this letter?" she demanded.

Dai looked at the identical letter he still had, and then back at his wife.

"Yes love. Why, what's wrong with it?"

Megan shook her head.

"You forgot to mention that we can also cater for parties and funerals. Sometimes I think if you were any thicker you would be bulletproof! Now start again - or if you want it done properly, pass it to me and I will do it."

Dai retrieved his pen and resumed writing as if he was a naughty schoolboy being given two hundred lines. He then passed it to Megan for approval. She nodded its improvement.

"Not too bad, Now you can go and talk to your friends if you want," as if he was a little lad being allowed out to play.

Two hours later Megan rang the bell for last orders. Just after eleven, as the locals started leaving, they handed Megan their letters for her to pass on to Mrs Morgan Morgan in the morning.

After the last customer had left Megan and Dai sat down and started to read the letters, looking out for really good ones and making sure that they had not written over the telephone number of their pub.

"Well. Fred Thomas is not going to be happy in the morning!" smiled Megan.

"What are you talking about, love?"

"Well, Freda's handed in his betting slip for tomorrow's race by mistake!"

"Come on love," Dai laughed. It's nearly quarter to twelve. Let's go to bed."

As Dai shut off the light off behind the bar Megan turned to him.

"Remember, it's not your birthday for another two months so don't get any funny ideas. Anyway I got a new book from the library today. It's called *Getting Away with Murder* so for your own health I suggest you don't try anything. But don't worry though: I got you a book too. It's called *Men Should Know Their Place in a Women's World*.

Dai looked at his wife in shock.

"Only joking, love. It's *Wales's Greatest Victories over England* in rugby, so it should take you about a month to read it. It should also keep you happy and your mind off other things as well."

And off they went to bed.

Dai smiled as he started to read the book. As a former amateur rugby player he loved reading anything about the sport but would never buy a book on it. 'Why buy one when you can rent one for nothing from a library?'

Chapter Three

From Brynlog to Brussels

Next morning Dai the Pub picked up the big brown manila envelope stuffed with letters from the kitchen table. He grabbed his coat and keys, and headed towards the Reverend Emmanuel's house. For the first time in a week the rain had ceased and the sun had emerged.

Dai stopped briefly and looked at the mountains surrounding the village: they seemed lush and green. He smiled in admiration. However many times he saw them, they always took his breath away. "God's country" he thought to himself.

Ten minutes later he walked up the Reverend's path. Standing at the door was Mrs Tompkins.

"Hello Dai the Pub. What is it you want on this fine morning?"

"I got the letters for the Reverend to take to the Brynlog Council," he smiled. "Is he here or somewhere else?"

"Well, he will either be here or somewhere else as he's got to be somewhere, hasn't he?"

Dai looked confused.

"OK, er...so is he here, then?"

"I don't know. Now I got here myself let's find out shall we?"

Mrs Tompkins got her key out of her handbag and opened the door. They both entered the hallway to be greeted by the sound of Reverend Emmanuel's voice singing along to an Aerosmith track on the radio.

"Hello Reverend Emmanuel," called Mrs Tompkins from just outside the kitchen door. She could not be heard as the Reverend saw neither Mrs Tompkins nor Dai standing there. He actually had his back to them and was now at full pelt singing "I don't want to miss a thing". Strangely, his deep tenor voice complemented Steven Tyler's higher range.

Mrs Tompkins tried again, to no avail, so Dai took his turn. Taking a deep breath, Dai shouted as loud as he could. It made Mrs Tompkins jump and scared the life out of the

Reverend so much so that he dropped his mug of coffee onto the floor.

"You stupid sod!" he exclaimed. "Dai, you have given me such a fright. The next funeral for me could have been my own!"

He shut off the radio.

"You also made me smash my favourite mug." he lamented, pointing to the pool of coffee all around the pieces. "I have had that mug since I was in Bible College over 50 years ago."

"Well at least it wasn't a new one then!" quipped Dai.

Mrs Tompkins tried to smother her laugh but failed. She quickly sought a brush and mop to clean it all up.

Mrs Ethel Tompkins was the Chairperson of the Chapel Sisterhood. This organisation was in charge of keeping the chapel clean and ensuring fresh flowers were in place for each Sunday sermon. They were so proud to have won the 'Best Kept Chapel' award twice in the last five years and always took pride in their work.

The chapel was also the only one in Wales that still had a wooden floor. After years of wear and tear the villagers started to express concern that the original stone floor was becoming uneven and wearing away. There were also two Reverends who had been buried under the stone floor over 200 years ago and unless something was done about it, they would have to be dug up and reburied in the churchyard.

After agreement from the Church of Wales a team of local carpenters were employed to place industrial laminated flooring on top of the original stone floor. It proved a great solution and the Sisterhood was highly delighted with it.

They also found it easier to maintain but had to curb their enthusiasm in the way they waxed it, particularly after an infamous incident two months before.

It occurred at the funeral for Mr Huw Thomas, the oldest villager. He had died in his sleep aged 92, his passing even making the first page of the local newspaper as well as the television. The Welsh news team had contacted the family a few days before the funeral to ask if they could have their permission to film it?

Such interest was generated by the fact that Huw Thomas had played for Wales in the Crown Green Bowls World Cup in 1965. He had been its captain, guiding them to runners' up position in the final. The news team promised to accord his funeral due dignity.

Three days before the funeral the Sisterhood had met to agree to polish and clean the chapel floor like never before, particularly if it was all going to be televised. They had even hired an industrial waxing machine from a shop in the village. After three hours of polishing, they left the floor to dry overnight, as instructed.

They returned the following morning but decided that it was really clean yet not good enough for the television. Undoubtedly other sisterhoods around Wales would be watching to see if they could spot any dirt or dust. So they decided to wax it once more.

The following day was the funeral of Mr Thomas, who made his final journey from the Co-op funeral parlour to the chapel and then onto his final resting place in the churchyard.

Mr Thomas had always said he wanted his final progression to be by a horse and carriage as he had lost a lot of his money on the horses over the years. "At least my horse will be first at the finishing line on that day!" he laughed.

The horses and funeral carriage pulled up outside the chapel gates. The horses were jet black and shone in the morning sun. The undertakers then removed the wreaths from the carriage, placing them just outside the chapel doors among other garlands already there. One of these came from the local bookmaker, whose simple message read 'Thanks for keeping us in business'. It brought a smile to all the mourners.

The cameras were already set up inside the chapel and would be started remotely from the crew's news van. Two cameras were positioned either side of the officiating Reverend Emmanuel's pulpit.

The sun was at its brightest and the reporter stood outside the chapel doors with a cameraman, relaying proceedings.

The bearers consisted of the six youngest choir members, complete with uniforms and wooden-soled shoes.

The choir master had chosen these for dramatic effect many years back so that when the choir were singing 'Onward Christian Soldiers', they would march on the spot for the audience to hear.

Mr Thomas was carried into the packed chapel towards the Reverend Emmanuel, already in position. The Reverend never walked in front of the coffin as he believed that you should never turn your back on the deceased: 'You should always watch them enter and welcome them with a bow.' Everyone attending the funeral should also bow as the coffin passed them.

The bearers had reached just ten yards down the aisle when the extremely waxed chapel floor and their wooden soles combined. The two front bearers slipped, falling backwards and bumping into the middle two bearers. They in turn slipped into the two bearers behind them and as they all fell down, the poor late Mr Thomas slid out of their hands.

The coffin itself was of highly polished oak which, upon making contact with the highly polished chapel floor, slid right up the aisle, only stopping as it hit the bottom of the two steps leading to Reverend Emmanuel's pulpit.

The procedural slow-bowing by the mourners as the deceased passed was now replaced by a sort of slowed down version of the type of head movement you saw at a Grand Prix.

The Reverend Emmanuel, never one to appear flustered, looked down at Mr Thomas and then back at the mourners. Without missing a beat the Reverend smiled, proclaiming,

"Well, at least he was not late for his own funeral. He made sure of that."

The whole chapel erupted with laughter as the six poor bearers struggled to their feet, regained their composure and very slowly walked up the aisle. They arrived at where Mr Thomas had come to a stop and picked up the coffin. He was finally placed upon the trestles originally intended. They then turned and were about to walk to their seats at the back of the chapel when the Reverend advised them to stand at the front for their own safety.

At the end of the service the bearers once again surrounded Mr Thomas's coffin. Yet this time they carried him out of the chapel using its handles as well as transporting the body at waist height, with one mourner at the front of the coffin, one at the back and the remaining four carrying him from the sides. It was one of the slowest funeral marches in history, taking almost five minutes to reach the chapel doors from the altar.

The remainder of the funeral passed without further incident but on the Welsh news that night it was once again shown for all of Wales to see. The Sisterhood would never live it down but on a lighter note, the Reverend's calmness and quip not only made the local newspaper but also the nationals, the headline reading 'High speed departures'. It made the Reverend a household name for at least a week but the Reverend made sure that an incident like that would never happen again.

His solution was to have one of the choir members walk up and down the aisle twice in their wooden-soled shoes before any service. This happened without fail whether it was for a marriage, funeral, christening or normal chapel service.

The Reverend put the kettle back on and offered Dai and Mrs Tompkins a fresh cup of coffee before they headed off to Mrs Morgan Morgan's house.

"Have you got enough cups for the three of us?" asked Dai, hoping that he would also see the funny side of it. The Reverend remained stone-faced while Dai sat down at the kitchen table waiting for Mrs Tompkins to finish cleaning up the mess and rejoin them.

"Well here they are, then!" announced Dai, picking up the brown manilla envelope he placed earlier upon the Reverend's kitchen table. "Megan and I went through all the letters last night after the pub closed and sorted out the silly and stupid ones from the proper ones. We filed the stupid ones under 'B' for safekeeping."

Mrs Tompkins, who had just joined them, looked a bit puzzled.

"What do you mean, Dai, you filed them under 'B'?. Surely they should be filed under 'S' for 'Stupid'."

Dai shook his head.

"No, you don't understand, mun. It's 'B' for 'bin'," he laughed.

"Oh, I see now," cried Mrs Tompkins, but both the Reverend and Dai knew she was just pretending and really did not understand.

"Well," exclaimed the Reverend after taking a big sup of his fresh hot steaming coffee. "It seems a bit pointless us reading them here and then once again over at Mrs Morgan Morgan's house as no doubt she will demand that we all pick the best ones together."

"You mean the ones that she likes? And we will all have to agree with her."

Both Mrs Tompkins and the Reverend nodded.

"That sounds more like it. Well, let's finish our cuppas and head off to the House of Horrors then."

This was one of Dai's more annoying habits: as soon as he thought of something funny he always started laughing before he finished his statement. Dai could never re-tell a joke he found really funny as he always laughed before the punchline. He consequently hardly ever completed any of his gags but always brightened up everyone's day, nonetheless, with his infectious laugh.

The three of them finished their coffees and after Mrs Tompkins had washed the mugs, they were ready to leave. The Reverend locked the door behind him and all three headed off to *that* house.

Walking down the chapel path Dai stopped to pay his respects to the grave of Mr Morgan, the last husband of Mrs Morgan Morgan.

"This is a man I admire for his bravery. Fancy marrying Mrs Morgan Morgan! He should have had a medal especially after she killed the other two off first."

Mrs Tompkins slapped Dai on his arm.

"You cannot say things like that in public! We all know that they died of natural causes. They were not murdered anyway. Mrs Morgan Morgan told us that."

"Well, reflected Dai, "I think that when she dies we should bury her next to the Bledwyn witch around the back so we can keep our eyes on them both at the same time!"

Ten minutes later they were at Mrs Morgan Morgan's gate. All of a sudden the sun hid behind grey clouds. Dai looked at the others:

"You're going to tell me that that's normal? That as we enter the House of Horrors that the sky turns from blue to black?! It's because you're a man of God and she is the Devil's daughter."

Mrs Tompkins shook her head.

"It could just be that we live in Wales and you can have all four seasons in an hour here."

"I suppose that could be the reason but if I was a betting man I would put my money on my explanation."

"If you were a betting man?" laughed the Reverend. "What do you mean? I often see you going in and out of Bryn the Bookies shop!"

"I only go in there to read the sports pages," Dai protested, "as Megan nags me if I sit in the bar reading them."

"Well, that's a pity you're not a betting man as only last week I was on the telephone to one of my fellow clergy and he was given a hot tip for the Grand National from one of his flock. He is so certain that it's going to win that he is going to put half the church roof fund on it."

"What is the name of the horse?" asked Dai with great curiosity.

"Well it's a bit pointless really telling you as you're not a betting man and I don't want to be the one to tempt you into gambling. As it says in The Lord's Prayer 'Lead us not into temptation'."

"Yes, yes but it also says that man cannot live by bread alone, doesn't it?"

"Fair point. I will try and remember the name for you. I mean just to satisfy your curiosity."

"Thank you Rev. As you know, they also say 'Curiosity killed the cat' and you don't want a death on your hands now, do you?"

The Reverend laughed.

"I tell you what I'll do," continued Dai. "I will pop over later with the names that have been announced as potential runners in the...er, what was the race called again? Oh, that's right: The Grand National."

Mrs Tompkins coughed.

"Any chance of us going in before it's time to go home?"

The three of them walked up the path and Mrs Tompkins rang the doorbell - which sounded like a cat being strangled. Dai immediately stood behind the other two and as the door opened, it started raining.

Mrs Morgan Morgan stood before them, as always dressed from head to toe in black.

"Damn. I must get a new battery for that doorbell. It normally plays that lovely tune, *O Fortuna*. Remind me to get new batteries when we're in Brynlog, please Mrs Tompkins. It's pointless asking a man to remember something that involves shopping as they always pretend to forget so they can get home quicker."

Mrs Morgan Morgan then walked down the passageway followed by Mrs Tompkins.

"Hang on Rev," requested Dai, grabbing his arm. "Isn't *O Fortuna* the theme tune to *The Exorcist* film?"

The Reverend nodded. Even he felt a cold shiver pass down his back before realising that Dai was standing right behind him, breathing heavily down his neck.

"For goodness sake, Dai! Pull yourself together, mun."

They followed Mrs Tompkins down the passageway and into Mrs Morgan Morgan's living room. Mrs Morgan Morgan told them to make themselves at home whilst she prepared the tea.

Reverend Emmanuel and Dai sat on the settee while Mrs Tompkins occupied one of the armchairs. No-one spoke but each knew what the other was thinking. Instead of a drab and dark living room, it was a lovely pastel shade with a two-seater cottage settee. There was one armchair at the end and another at the other, all complemented by a light oak coffee table in the middle accommodating a fresh bunch of flowers.

"We have been bewitched," Dai whispered. "It's all in our imagination. If we wake up we will find ourselves in a dungeon and she will be mixing rats' tails and eyes of newts in a cauldron. Quick. Rev, pinch me!"

The Reverend decided to teach Dai a lesson - and pinched him as hard as he could. The shock made Dai jump up and yelp.

"What you doing, mun? That hurt that did. Is there something wrong with you, you div [stupid person]?"

Dai was rubbing his arm when the living room door opened and in came Mrs Morgan Morgan with the tea and biscuits on a tray. She looked at Dai nursing his arm.

"What's the matter with you, David the Public House?" Dai had to think quickly.

"I got cramp in my arm."

Mrs Morgan Morgan looked puzzled.

"Well, in all my years in the medical profession I have never heard or come across someone with cramp in their arm. You must be a medical marvel."

"Well," panicked Dai, "it started off in my leg but it travelled up to my arm. It's due to…when I was down the mine and also being in the pub trade. Cold and dark in the mine and cold and dark in my cellar. It's called 'Mine-barrel Syndrome'" he smiled, hoping to impress her.

Mrs Morgan Morgan looked back at Dai. She was not convinced. The Reverend realised that this could develop into a full investigation and decided to help Dai out. After all, it was partly his fault.

"Well, Mrs Morgan Morgan. Last night Megan and Dai went through and sorted out the letters ready to present to Brynlog Council."

He patted the brown manilla envelope Dai had put on the coffee table as if to show her the proof. Mrs Morgan Morgan sighed deeply.

"Reverend Ivor Emmanuel, you silly man! We are not going to see any councillor: we are going to see the Mayor!"

Mrs Tompkins nearly choked on her tea and placed the cup back on the saucer.

"I did not know we had an appointment with the Mayor?" blurted Mrs Tompkins. "When did you make the appointment? I thought he would be too busy to see us. You're very lucky."

Mrs Morgan Morgan put up her hand.

"My dear Mrs Tompkins. I have not made an appointment but when he finds out that I wish to speak to him he will cancel all his other appointments especially for me, I can assure you. I was the matron when he was born and I also nursed his mother 20 years later when she was ill. So, he will remember me and as I said he will cancel everything else when he's informed of our arrival. Now let's finish our tea quickly as there's a Mayor to terrorise this morning!"

Mrs Morgan Morgan took the tray out and Dai looked at the others.

"See," he said. "She is going to terrorise the Mayor. We will be arrested, tried as terrorists and then sent to Guantanamo Bay."

Mrs Tompkins looked puzzled.

"Is that near Swansea?"

Dai shook his head.

"No, that's Bracelet Bay. Guantanamo Bay is near Mexico."

"Oh, that's fine. I don't have a passport so I won't be allowed to go."

The Reverend shook his head at the pair of them.

"She's not going to blow him up. She's just going to gently persuade him."

The door opened slightly and in wandered straight up to Dai a jet black cat. It just sat there, licked his lips, its green eyes seeming to look inside the soul of Dai. The Reverend watched Dai freeze in terror. He could not speak, his eyes transfixed by the cat's stare.

Suddenly Mrs Morgan Morgan returned, spotted the cat and walked over to pick it up.

"Mr Fluffy. I have told you a thousand times you're not allowed in here when we have guests."

Mr Fluffy duly hissed at Dai as he was gently removed.

"Well, that cured my constipation!" Dai thought to himself.

Mrs Tompkins looked puzzled.

"I just thought to myself, how are we going to get to Brynlog? None of us have fetched our cars, it's too far to walk and the bus does not run either today."

Dai rose.

"I will walk back to the *Drag and Daff* and get mine." As he started towards the door Mrs Morgan Morgan re-appeared. Once again he felt his heart beat faster.

"I'm...I'm going to get my car," he stuttered. "Won't be long!"

Mrs Morgan Morgan smiled.

"You don't have to. We will go in mine."

"Well in that case, asked Dai, "can I use your toilet please? It's an emergency."

Mrs Morgan Morgan informed him that the bathroom was at the top of the stairs and also that she did not have a toilet, she had a "bathroom".

Dai ascended the stairs quickly. Ten minutes later they were outside Mrs Morgan Morgan's garage waiting for her to drive out her car.

"I did not even know she had a car, Mrs Tompkins," laughed Dai. "I bet it's a batmobile."

The Reverend looked puzzled.

"What do you mean: a 'batmobile'?"

"Work it out, replied Dai. "Being a witch she would have a *bat*mobile, wouldn't she?"

Mrs Tompkins told them both to be quiet. "I can hear her coming."

The garage doors opened sideways. There before them, in all its glory, was a 1970 Morris Minor. It looked as new now as it did all those years ago: beige in colour with matching wheel trims.

"Where do you get parts for that, Mrs Morgan Morgan?" enquired Dai. "Brynlog museum?" he laughed.

Mrs Morgan Morgan looked him straight in the eye.

"Let me tell you David the Public House. This car runs the same as it did when it first came out of the garage. It's more reliable than most of the rubbish on the roads these days. They knew how to make them then. Now, get in you lot: there's a Mayor we have to see!"

The Morris burst into life on the first turn of the key. Even Dai was impressed but said nothing. The car chugged its way onto Lower High Street bound for Brynlog. The Reverend sat in the front passenger seat, with Mrs Tompkins and Dai occupying the back.

"I see you don't have any seatbelts back here," Mrs Tompkins queried to Mrs Morgan Morgan.

"When this car was made there was no need for any seatbelts to be fitted at the back," she retorted. "Everyone drove sensibly and also you had none of those happy riders in their stewed-up cars either."

Mrs Tompkins looked at Dai for a explanation.

"She means 'joyriders' in 'souped-up' cars," laughed Dai.

The Reverend stared at the pair of them.

"Let me tell you, Mrs Morgan Morgan is right. I can remember when in the good old days you could leave your car unlocked. If you were a member of the AA and passed an AA patrol man and he saw your AA badge, he would salute you out of respect. No-one ever went faster than 50 miles per hour and also you did not have all the mod-cons like air-conditioning or really bright lights. If it was foggy you did not go out and the windows were your air-conditioner."

The Reverend turned back around but continued talking.

"All you had to do was just turn the handle - like this." The Reverend turned the window handle slightly upon which the window dropped straight down into its housing. He looked at Mrs Morgan Morgan in sheer terror. Mrs Morgan Morgan slammed on the brakes on and glared at the Reverend.

"Did I say you could play with it?"

"I'm sorry Mrs Morgan Morgan," came his sheepish reply. "I don't know my own strength."

Mrs Morgan Morgan exited the vehicle and walked to the passenger side.

"Well, it might be old but the electric windows are fast!" quipped Dai to the Reverend.

Opening the passenger door wide, Mrs Morgan Morgan gently pulled off its backing and pushed the window back up without saying a word. She then walked back to the driver's side and put on her seatbelt.

"Now, Reverend. Can you keep your hands to yourself please, if you don't mind?"

For the rest of the journey the Reverend just sat there with his arms folded. By the time they arrived at Brynlog he had cramp in both of them.

The car pulled into Brynlog County Council car park 40 minutes later. Mrs Morgan Morgan pulled into a reserved parking space and shut off the engine.

"We can't park here!" exclaimed the Reverend. "We are not 'Staff' are we?"

Mrs Morgan Morgan shrugged her shoulders.

"Well they should have got to work earlier then, to get their parking space. As they say, 'The early bird catches the worm'."

The three of them disembarked and Mrs Morgan Morgan locked the doors. She then straightened her hat and with her bag over her lower arm, started marching towards the old oak doors that led to Brynlog Council's office. Her companions sauntered behind her like naughty school children.

The receptionist was in the middle of a telephone conversation when they arrived. Mrs Morgan Morgan duly waited for ten seconds and then rang the bell twice – which just happened to be situated on the same desk as the phone. The receptionist looked up.

"Excuse me madam!" she cried. "Can't you see I'm on the phone? I will be with you in one moment."

She continued with her conversation. Mrs Morgan Morgan growled back.

"How dare you! Don't you know who I am?"

The receptionist looked at her once more.

"Sorry Tina. I will ring you back. I got a woman here with amnesia. She can't remember who she is!"

She put the phone back and put on her best insincere smile.

"Yes madam. How may I help you?"

Mrs Morgan Morgan lent towards her.

"First of all, I have never worked or owned a house of ill repute, so I am not a 'madam'. The name is 'Mrs Morgan Morgan'."

Mrs Tompkins mouthed to Dai, "House of ill repute?" Dai mouthed back the word "brothel". Mrs Tompkins giggled then pretended to cough causing Mrs Morgan Morgan to redirect her stare. Regaining her composure, she proclaimed,

"You may tell the Mayor I am here and waiting to see him."

"Do you have an appointment ma...?"

She stopped short of calling her 'madam' realising that it could prompt another tirade.

"Do you have an appointment, Mrs Morgan Morgan?"

"I do not need an appointment young lady. Once he knows I'm here he will put everything else aside to see me."

The receptionist smiled.

"I'm sorry but you can only see him if you have an appointment like every other normal person."

At this point Mrs Morgan Morgan's voice reverted to her matron tones.

"Listen! I am not 'a normal person' so I don't need an appointment."

With that Dai tapped Mrs Tompkin's shoulder: "Told you she wasn't normal!"

Mrs Tompkins this time, however, could not contain her laughter. As it echoed through the hallway the Reverend and Mrs Morgan Morgan looked at her in disgust.

"I'm sorry," she lied, "I just remembered something funny from television last night. I will be quiet from now on."

Once they had looked away again, she hit Dai in the stomach whilst mouthing "You div" at him.

Mrs Morgan Morgan meanwhile refused to give in to the receptionist.

"Could you please tell the Mayor that I'm here to see him? And hurry up about it! Let me tell you, if you had been a nurse on my ward when I was in charge, you would have been out the door so quickly your feet would have not touched the ground!"

Fearing total lack of progress here, the Reverend decided to intervene and so tapped Mrs Morgan Morgan on the shoulder: "Let me try please." Moving forward he smiled at the receptionist.

"Excuse me young lady. May I introduce myself? I am the Reverend Ivor Emannuel. Would you please try and see if you can get in touch with the Mayor so that we may present him with a petition from the village of Aberglas?"

He then pointed to a row of chairs along the wall to his left. They would not have looked out of place in a museum.

"We will sit over there whilst we wait for you to hopefully get in touch with His Worship The Mayor."

The Reverend gestured to the others to follow him. The receptionist pressed one of the buttons on her keypad. After a brief conversation she replaced the receiver.

The Reverend, Mrs Tompkins, Mrs Morgan Morgan and Dai were still sitting on the chairs bolt upright, Mrs Morgan Morgan with her large black large handbag on her lap with both hands clutching it whilst the Reverend had closed his eyes as if in prayer to a higher authority.

Mrs Tompkins and Dai looked around to see if anything was happening. They had been there for less than five minutes when Mrs Morgan Morgan stood up and walked back over to the receptionist.

"I have been sitting over there for 30 minutes. How long does it take for you to contact him? It's only the Mayor, not God for goodness sake!"

"I will have you know that I just tried to contact him but the office number is engaged at the moment. I will try again in a minute. Did you say you are a retired matron, Mrs Morgan Morgan?"

"I am but I don't understand what that has to do with you getting in touch with the Mayor?" snapped the latter.

"Well, in that case you should have more patients [patience]."

Her joke failed to elicit a smile. Instead Mrs Morgan Morgan merely resumed her seat.

The receptionist tried once more to contact the Mayor's office but without success. By chance, at that moment a smartly dressed man entered the building and walked straight up to her. It was Councillor Thomas Jenkins.

"Hello Jenny, how are you this morning?" he beamed.

"I'm very well thank you Mr Jenkins."

Jenny then picked up a paper from her desk and read it to him.

"Mr Lewis, your first appointment has rung and apologised. Due to circumstances beyond his control he cannot make the meeting with you this morning."

"Oh well," he sighed. "At least I have a chance to catch up on my paperwork now. Thank you for letting me know."

Suddenly Mrs Morgan Morgan rose from her chair.

"Excuse me," she bellowed.

"Er, hello may I help you?" he replied, slightly startled.

"I'm Mrs Morgan Morgan. What is your position here, may I ask?"

"I'm the Deputy Mayor of Brynlog" he smiled proudly.

If Thomas had known what was coming he would have said he was someone else.

"Well in that case your paperwork is going to have to wait, now. I would like you to show us to your office so we can have a nice friendly little chat."

She gestured to the others to follow her to Thomas' office.

"Er...well, please come in and make yourselves comfortable," offered Mr Jenkins. "I will just order us some refreshments. Is tea OK for everyone?"

They all accepted so he phoned for the drinks. Dai and the Reverend brought in two chairs from outside and joined the ladies now sitting opposite Thomas' desk.

"Well then. How may I help you today?" smiled Thomas.

"Well, we are the Chapel Council from Aberglas so I assume you know why we are here?" commenced Mrs Morgan Morgan.

"I'm sorry, I have no idea what you are talking about. Could you please enlighten me?"

Mrs Morgan Morgan glanced at the Reverend.

"I knew we should have waited for the Mayor instead of his tea boy!"

"If you would tell me your reason for being here I'm sure I can help you somehow," Thomas retorted.

Mrs Morgan Morgan took out from her bag the Council's original letter to the Reverend regarding the twinning proposal.

"We are here about this!" handing Mr Jenkins the letter.

"OK," resumed Thomas upon absorbing its contents, "what seems to be the problem? It all seems easy and straight forward enough to me. Can I just say that we just don't pick a name out of a hat, you know. There is a lot of thought and planning that goes into twinning towns."

"Well, we are not happy about it. If we are going to be forced into twinning with another town it should be our choice, not yours!"

Thomas did not move.

"Listen," she continued. "We live in Aberglas. How would you like it if we chose a twin town for Brynlog without asking you? I have the perfect place for you: it's Transylvania, where the other bloodsuckers live!"

Dai pulled his collar up over his neck. Thomas looked at Mrs Morgan Morgan.

"I hope you're not implying that we at Brynlog Council are bloodsuckers? We are chosen and elected on the grounds that we are honest and care about the people who voted for us, I will have you know."

"That might work on television but it does not work on us. We want you lot to cancel this ridiculous idea and leave us alone or face the wrath of God upon you!"

Thomas looked shocked. About to reply he was interrupted by a knock at the door. In walked a woman in white blouse and black skirt carrying a tray of tea and biscuits. Thomas thanked her and she left.

Dai the Pub passed the tray around and then replaced it. Thomas picked up his cup and saucer which rattled loudly in his shaking hands. He quickly put it back on the table.

"Are you feeling all right?" asked the Reverend. "You look a bit pale."

"No, I'm fine thank you," he coughed.

He looked once more at Mrs Morgan Morgan.

"I must ask you, Mrs Morgan Morgan. Are you threatening me and my fellow councillors?"

Mrs Morgan Morgan smiled.

"I do not threaten, Mr Jenkins. I make promises. You can ask anyone who knows me that."

Dai starting nodding furiously. Thomas returned his attention to Mrs Morgan Morgan.

"I must inform you that threatening a member of Brynlog Council can get you arrested. Do you understand that?"

Mrs Morgan Morgan smiled.

"Have I threatened you? I don't think so. And where are your witnesses to this so-called 'threat'? Did any of you three hear me threaten him?"

She glanced back at the others. They all shook their heads.

"Never heard anything," piped Dai, "and I have been here all the time."

Thomas realised that his threat was about as much use as a handbrake on a canoe. He therefore decided to get back on their good side.

"I'm sure that we can work out the best solution for both sides," he smiled.

Mrs Morgan Morgan stood up and looked him straight in the eye.

"I see you have come to your senses. At last I agree with you that a solution for both sides would be best. So the best solution is to stop this stupid idea and leave us alone, you silly little jumped-up bureaucrat!"

She resumed her chair.

Thomas picked up the phone; his hand was shaking.

"I need security here, now please to escort four people from my office as soon as possible."

Two minutes later Thomas' door burst open with three men in white shirts and black ties. The word 'Security' adorned their hats.

"Please escort these people from my office immediately and ensure they are removed from the premises completely," he trembled.

The four of them stood up.

"You have not heard the end of this boyo," threatened the Reverend.

Mrs Morgan Morgan strode towards the security men.

"Get out of my way!"

They quickly complied. Dai stretched out to shake Thomas' hand.

"Thanks for the tea, butte. It was tidy."

Thomas robotically took his hand, and as Dai left he remained immobile, his hand still outstretched like a mannequin. Escorted down the corridor Mrs Morgan Morgan turned to one of the guards.

"Wow!" Your mother will be so proud of you saving a defenceless man from a retired matron, a Reverend, the Chairperson of the Sisterhood and a retired miner."

The guard continued to marshal them out of the building.

"Do you have any transport situated in our car park?"

Mrs Morgan Morgan stared at him contemptuously.

"Of course we have! You don't think we walked here, young man?! It's over there," pointing to her little Morris Minor occupying the staff car bay.

"Do you not know that you are parked illegally?"

The Reverend considered the guard asking the question.

"What are you going to do then? Make us repark somewhere else before you force us to leave?"

"You can park anywhere you like as long as it's not on this property. Now please leave before we have to get the police involved - which I'm sure you don't want to happen, do you?"

Mrs Morgan Morgan rounded on him at this.

"Are there any real men working here at all? All I have seen is you all hide behind each other and threaten a poor old widow woman and her friends with arrest. Could I just say this to you that a stint in the Army would do you lot the world of good. Let me tell you it might make men of you!"

With that she turned towards her car smiling, knowing she again had had the last word. As she started the car Dai suggested to the others that they should go to the Brynlog Inn for something to eat and plan their next assault. To his amazement they immediately agreed.

Twenty minutes later the four of them were sitting in its lounge with Dai nursing a pint of bitter. Dai the Inn joined them.

"So, what's the problem then my friends?"

Dai the Pub relayed the story.

"Hang on," ventured Dai the Inn upon its conclusion, "let me get my laptop. I got something to show you and I'm sure it will help."

Dai charged the device and typed 'little village wins fight against government' into his Google tab. Google duly responded with exactly what Dai the Inn wanted:

'The village of Killesberg in France after a short legal battle, won its case today against the proposal to twin it with another town.

'Killesberg's Mayor took their appeal to the High Court and after he presented the court with a five-thousand named petition and a fully documented report from the village stating how it would not be welcomed, the High Court ruled in Killesberg's favour, quashing the twinning Killesberg with another town against their will.'

Dai the Inn beamed at the four of them.

"There you go. That's your answer there in black and white!"

Mrs Tompkins spoke up first.

"So we have to go to Killesberg to meet the Mayor and ask him for their help, do we?"

The Reverend shook his head in despair.

"No, he won't help us. We need to find a different European High Court. Don't think we should go to the same one as Killesberg did."

"You need to go to Brussels," suggested Dai the Inn, "to the court of Human Rights. They are the ones who will help you."

The Reverend appeared bemused.

"Why?"

"I saw a documentary on television about it. They are in charge of all European issues these days."

Mrs Morgan Morgan shook her head.

"It's no wonder we are in a mess. We are being looked after by a bunch of sprout growers."

After an hour the four of them had finished their drinks. They thanked Dai for his hospitality and headed back to Aberglas. During the journey they agreed to arrange another meeting about going to Brussels and representing the village in their fight against the enemy, Brynlog Council. All four decided to put up notices in all the shops, the Chapel and *The Dragon and Daff* when they had a date.

Chapter Four

On the march to Europe

Four days later, at 7pm once again the village hall was packed. This time it was a more relaxed atmosphere. Mrs Morgan Morgan, Dai the Pub and the Reverend Ivor Emmanuel were seated on the stage.

Mrs Morgan Morgan stood up and raised her hand. The crowd fell silent.

"Thank you ladies and gentleman for attending this emergency meeting against the oppression of the enemy arising in the distance."

Some of the crowd, including poor Mrs Tompkins, looked puzzled at this opening statement. So Dai the Pub also rose to his feet.

"What Mrs Morgan Morgan is trying to say is that those idiots in Brynlog won't change their minds about the twinning. But we got an idea!"

"That's what I just said, didn't I?" glared Mrs Morgan back at Dai. "David the Public House took us to meet with a fellow publican in Brynlog after the disgraceful way were we treated by Councillor Thomas Jenkins," his name pronounced through gritted teeth, "...after the way we were mistreated, we took refuge afterwards by going for some light refreshments." She then turned to Dai. "Is that better? Can you understand now what I'm saying?"

"You're doing OK. Please continue."

Mrs Morgan Morgan did precisely that.

"When David the Brynlog Inn joined us, he brought with him a tabletop computer."

Dai burst out laughing. Mrs Morgan Morgan threw him back an evil stare.

"What's so funny?"

"It's called a laptop not a tabletop!"

She remained fixed on him.

"And where exactly was the computer when he showed us the story?"

"In the lounge," he replied.

"No. I mean *what* did he place the computer on?"
Dai looked puzzled: "It was on the table."
"There we go then," smiled Mrs Morgan Morgan. "So it's a tabletop computer. Now please be quiet! Anymore outbursts and you will be removed from the stage."
Dai now sat there with his arms folded, his face pouting.
"As I was saying," continued Mrs Morgan Morgan, "he showed us that a little village in France had beaten the oppressors… I mean…" rapidly changing her words, "their local council. So we have therefore decided to go to Brussels in Europe to show them they can't mess with us either!"
The crowd started clapping enthusiastically until Mrs Morgan Morgan once more raised her hand for some quiet.
"To do this," she continued proudly, "we need everyone's help. We can't do it alone." She gestured towards the Reverend and Dai. "We may be three like the three musketeers but even they had help from a fourth. So you are going to be our dog-man-tan."
Dai the Pub burst out laughing once again.
"It's 'D'artagnan'. He was French."
"Does it matter?" interrupted the Reverend. "We are going to Brussels, not France anyway."
"Never mind," sighed Dai and beckoned Mrs Morgan Morgan's to continue.
"Thank you David the Public House. If it's OK with you I will carry on."
Dai nodded his agreement.
"This time…this time…"
Dai pulled a face he thought had made Mrs Morgan Morgan smile. The real reason, however, for her improved demeanour was the knowledge that she had won her argument with Dai.
"We have come up," she pursued, "with a battle plan. But first of all we need to raise money for the flights to Brussels and also for the return journey, plus a hotel."
Sian the Shop raised her hand at this point.
"What is it, Sian the Newspaper Shop?"
Sian stood up.

"If we are all going to Brussels we will need to hire our own big plane to ensure we all get there the same time and on the right flight. We would not want to end up in Brazil instead of Brussels now, would we?"

"I wouldn't mind ending up in Brazil," piped Dai. "Have you seen those Brazilian women. Woo wee!"

At this Megan threw him a dirty look. Yet her husband, always one for thinking on his feet, merely smiled, continuing:

"As I said, those Brazilian women are pretty - but not as pretty as my Megan!"

Megan's expression suggested that Dai was still in a hole of his own making.

"As I said," persisted Sian, "I will need to know the date as I'm going to have to close the shop."

Here Mrs Morgan Morgan interrupted.

"I'm sorry Sian the Newspaper Shop. You seem to have misunderstood what I said. It's only going to be the Reverend, David the Public House and myself going to Brussels to represent Aberglas."

This sent a murmur all around the hall.

"I am aware that this sounds like a little holiday to you but I can assure you that there will be no fun to be had!"

"Not with her coming," mouthed Dai to the Reverend, tapping him on the arm. The Reverend nodded, undetected in agreement.

"There were going to be four of us originally visiting Brussels but Mrs Tompkins is waiting for a hospital appointment and does not want to risk missing it. She has been on the waiting for almost two years and can be called in anytime. So it's just the three of us instead.

"Now, before we even think of going to Brussels we will need at least a thousand-name petition to present to the court. And before you say anything, I know there are only 526 people living in the village after the death of Mr Thomas."

As ever Mrs Morgan Morgan had given the exact figure.

"So you will all need to ask family and friends from other places to sign our petition. Also we need as many as we can get.

"Next on the agenda," she breezed, looking down at her piece of paper, "is raising funds. We could have the usual fundraisers: fête or bric-a-brac et cetera but we need to raise funds quicker than that."

"The Reverend told me that he has a hot tip for the Grand National. Now if we all put a tenner on it we will get the money for the trip easily!" interjected Dai.

"I was just joking, mun. Just wanted to see if you would admit to going into the bookies to bet!"
Dai looked crestfallen.

"I can't believe a man of the cloth would lie, raising all my hopes...er, I mean, raising all *our* hopes." Looking at Megan the correction was too late. "That's another fine mess you've got yourself into, you div," he thought to himself.

Mrs Morgan Morgan tutted at his own goal.

"Now let's get back to how to raise this money. We need to finance the trip. Any ideas are welcome as long as they are sensible. We will need to stay at least one night in Brussels in case we have to see more than one person. And just in case we don't get the answer we are looking for from the first person we will not roll over and die: we are the original Aberglas people and we will never be twinned with any phoney Aberglas!"

This time Mrs Morgan Morgan received a standing ovation. When it finally ceased Paula the Post raised her hand.

"Yes Paula the Post Office. What is your idea?"

"Do we have any money in the chapel roof fund?" enquired Paula, now standing.

"I will have to check one moment," replied the
Reverend. "I will have to go to the vestry and bring back the ledger. I will be back as soon as I can. Meanwhile, please carry on."

The Reverend headed out of the hall. Awaiting his return other ideas were discussed, some stupid and some really stupid like sponsored car washes and people paying to have their gardens watered and weeded. Dai pointed out that 'it was Wales, mun, and it rains nearly every day here so God washes and waters our cars and gardens for free'.

The Reverend returned 20 minutes later with the chapel ledger in hand. Retrieving his spectacles from his inside pocket, and then placing them on his head, he opened it. Mrs Morgan Morgan did her usual trick of raising her hand to quieten the crowd.

"You may report the finances now, Reverend."

"Up to yesterday," commenced the Reverend, "we have a grand total for the chapel roof fund of £727.36p."

"Well, that should cover some of the cost of the trip without any problem," declared Mrs Morgan Morgan.

"I agree but I'm a bit nervous spending it. What happens if the chapel roof comes off and we have used up all the money?"

"Don't be such a Babi-lol [cry baby]. The chapel has been there for hundreds of years and I'm sure will stay on for a bit longer. And anyway the £727 won't be enough anyway."

Dai looked at Mrs Morgan Morgan:

"You forgot the 36 pence."

After a show of hands it was agreed that the money would be used to fund the trip. It was also agreed that everyone at the meeting would donate £10 each to ensure the full cost of the trip was covered. At its conclusion Mrs Morgan Morgan requested everyone to sign individual petition forms on their way out.

"We need different names. Please try and achieve this as soon as possible."

She closed the meeting at 8.36pm, minuted for future reference. Once again Dai announced that the pub would be open thinking it a good idea for everyone to relax after such an intense meeting. This did the trick, with most of the crowd heading off to the *Dragon and Daff* including this time Mrs Morgan Morgan and the Reverend.

Upon arrival Dai, Mrs Morgan Morgan and the Reverend headed to the quiet of the lounge to finalise the details. Dai treated himself to a pint of lager whilst Mrs Morgan Morgan had a small sherry; the Reverend, however, much to Dai and Mrs Morgan Morgan's amazement enjoyed a large white wine. The Reverend explained that most wine is blessed in chapel. He then made a cross over the glass and took a big gulp of it.

With pen and paper Dai started making a list of all the things they needed to do. The top priority was to go to Brynlog and find a travel agency selling flights to Brussels and hotel rooms near enough to the Court of Human Rights. It was agreed that the three of them would do this next morning. They would then be able to take on Europe and surely come home triumphant.

Dai smiled. "Do you realise in years to come that people will read about our victory on the internet – which, of course, will be much more poignant."

"Why more poignant than that of Killesberg?" queried the Reverend.

Dai explained that they would have left Wales and travelled abroad, beating the enemy in their own back garden despite their real enemy's back garden being Brynlog - only ten miles away.

At exactly 9am next day Mrs Morgan Morgan's Morris Minor pulled up outside the *Dragon and Daff*, having already picked up The Reverend. Dai waved to the pair of them but had no response.

"Thanks for waving back to me."

"You only wave Goodbye. You don't wave Hello. You *say* 'Hello'."

Arriving about 40 minutes later in Brynlog, they sought the travel agency. In walked the 'three musketeers', as Dai had decided to call them. The shop was just a small independent premise. From behind her computer on the front desk, a young girl smiled a "Good morning, I'm Michelle. How may I help you?"

Mrs Morgan Morgan smiled back.

"At least you're nicer than the other receptionist we met here."

I'm sorry? I am actually a travel advisor not a receptionist."

The three sat down. Mrs Morgan Morgan occupied the middle, as always with her big black handbag on her lap.

"We are going to Brussels to take on the powers-that-be. Now, when can you get us there and also as we will need to stay there overnight we will need three separate rooms, obviously?"

Dai put his arm around Mrs Morgan Morgan.

"I thought this was going to be a romantic trip, darling."

If looks could kill he would now be lying next to the Bledwyn Witch in the graveyard. Dai retracted his arm.

"Sorry! Just trying to lighten the mood."

Michelle smiled. "Let me check."

She started inputting their request and after a few minutes looked at the three of them.

"You can fly from Cardiff International Airport with 'Fly Us' airline, staying at the Brussels Hilton for one night, breakfast included, for £295 each."

The Reverend coughed.

"It's only one night we want!"

"The cost is extra because you all want separate rooms," explained Michelle.

Dai lent towards Michelle.

"How much would it be then if we shared – that is, the Reverend and me - not *her*?" glancing gingerly towards Mrs Morgan Morgan.

"It would then be £600 for all three of you: one single and one twin room plus breakfast," replied Michelle, once more consulting her computer.

"How about then if we don't have breakfast? It's going to be continental anyway as we're abroad and we could always find a café nearby for some proper food."

Anticipating Dai's question Michelle explained that it would then cost £510 for the three of them. Dai winked at Michelle.

"And if we walked instead of flying?"

Only Michelle and Dai laughed at his joke.

"David the Public House! Will you please be sensible? Otherwise you will not be coming with us," snapped Mrs Morgan Morgan. Dai felt like a child being grounded for naughtiness.

"We will have some refreshments and return when we have made our decision," declared Mrs Morgan Morgan to Michelle. "But before we go, can you confirm to us when we would be able to go to Brussels?"

Michelle looked again.

"There's a flight available on Thursday and also two rooms available at the Brussels Hilton that day."

Mrs Morgan Morgan exited the travel agency, bound for the tea rooms across the road. There they agreed Michelle's suggestions. Dai opened his inside pocket.

"Bet you thought I had forgotten my passport? But I'm not as dumb as I look," he smiled.

The Reverend laughed:

"No-one could be that dumb!"

Dai's smile turned to a frown. Then the Reverend similarly retrieved his passport from inside his coat.

"Got mine, too."

Mrs Morgan Morgan looked at the pair of them.

"Why have you got your passports with you? We do not need them. We are staying in Europe."

"We are flying out of Britain. We need a passport. Don't say you don't have one?"

Mrs Morgan Morgan looked Dai straight in the eye.

"Of course I have one. I had one when I married Mr Thomas. We were going to go on honeymoon to America. Then the Vietnam war started and we decided we did not want to be there in case the Vietnamese invaded America."

"When did you get it?" Dai asked.

Mrs Morgan Morgan thought for a moment.

"1967."

The Reverend smiled.

"I think you need to renew it then as it might be a little out of date."

"This is so stupid! I can go to four countries without a passport but I need one to go to Brussels?"

"What four countries can you go to without a passport?" Dai enquired looking puzzled.

"Well I can go to England, Scotland, the Isle of Wight and Ireland without one."

"No you can't. You can only go to Northern Ireland. You need a passport for Southern Ireland. That's in Europe now."

"That is so stupid!" retorted Mrs Morgan Morgan. "That's like Aberglas being in Britain and Swansea being in Europe!"

"They were in Europe once." Dai ventured. "European Cup Winners Cup 1981. I saw them win 12 nil down The Vetch but I had a bet on the other side to win."

"It's no wonder you don't bet anymore," quipped the Reverend tapping Dai on the shoulder. "Now let's go back to the travel agents and find out how long it will take to get you a passport Mrs Morgan Morgan."

"So you decided then? smiled Michelle. "Shall I book it for Thursday?"

"Slight problem," replied Dai awkwardly. The three of them sat down. "Mrs Morgan Morgan has a slight issue with her passport. We think it might be a little out of date."

Michelle looked at Mrs Morgan Morgan.

"They last ten years these days, you know. When did you last renew it?" she enquired, turning to Mrs Morgan Morgan.

"1967."

Michelle looked shocked.

"My mother wasn't even born then!" she exclaimed.

This did not ease the situation. Michelle then told them she had an idea: she would dial the Passport Office in Newport.

Shortly she replaced the receiver. If they all went there it would only take a week. However, if they told them that it was an official visit, they could rush it through and have it the same day. Michelle smiled, continuing:

"Would you like me to reserve your airline tickets and rooms anyway? If you don't go you can have all your deposits back."

They immediately agreed, paid Michelle the money, thanked her and left. Mrs Morgan Morgan's Morris Minor was now bound for Newport.

Two hours later they found themselves in the Passport Office waiting room. Mrs Morgan Morgan filled in the paperwork and then went to have her passport photo taken. Dai stood on the other side of the short curtain as she sat there reading the instructions.

"I know it will be hard for you but try not to smile as they don't like it!" ordered Dai bursting into laughter.

Mrs Morgan Morgan's umbrella appeared from under the curtain and poked Dai straight in the shin. Dai hopped away, cursing her under his breath.

They then all waited to be called. They were number '99', with '85' already showing.

"Think we will only be here for about half an hour," surmised Dai.

Two hours later the counter finally clicked over to '99'. Mrs Morgan Morgan disappeared into the cubicle and after another 30 minutes re-emerged.

"We will have to wait another two hours. Then it will be ready."

"Well in that case," declared Dai, "I'm off for a walk. I can't sit here another two hours. You coming, Rev? I know of a lovely church just around the corner. We could go and visit?"

The Reverend was rather shocked that Dai knew of a church and wanted to visit it as well.

"Yes. Of course I will accompany you," he offered.

They looked at Mrs Morgan Morgan.

"You joining us?"

"Unlike you two I have plenty of patience so I'm quite comfortable here!" she retorted.

"Well that's what you get for being a matron in a hospital for over a century: 'Patients'."

He moved quickly away remembering the shin poke earlier.

The Reverend and Dai stood up and left to visit the church. Mrs Morgan Morgan kept her usual pose.

"This way," Dai instructed the Reverend.

After five minutes they turned down a side road. The Reverend stopped.

"Are you sure there's a church around here?" queried the Reverend.

"Yes. It's just up a bit."

"Well I think we are on the wrong road as I can't see a steeple," replied the Reverend scanning the sky.

"There we go! I told you I knew where I was going" exclaimed Dai as they stood outside *The Old Church* public house. The Reverend looked at Dai in disgust.

"Well it used to be a church. Come on. We are here now."

They walked up to the bar and waited to be served. There were about ten or so people in there, some watching the racing on the television, while others read their newspapers. The landlord approached through the door behind the bar.

"Good afternoon, gents. What can I get you?"

Dai looked at the beer pumps.

"I will have a pint of lager please. What you having then, Rev?"

The landlord laughed. "I know we are called *The Old Church* but there was no need to dress as a vicar and be called 'Rev'!"

Dai looked at the landlord.

"Actually he is a real Reverend and this is not fancy dress I can assure you."

The colour drained from the landlord's face.

"I'm so sorry. I did not mean to offend you. I thought it was a joke. Please accept my apology and the drinks are on me! Now, what was it again? A pint of Lager and a..?"

Dai interrupted.

"Sorry. Did I say 'Pint of lager'? I meant a double vodka and coke."

The landlord stared at Dai.

"Fair enough. Double vodka and coke."

"I will have a large glass of wine," corrected the Reverend.

The landlord looked at the Reverend.

"Are you sure you're not winding me up?"

The Reverend took out his bank card from his wallet and handed it to him. The card clearly stated 'Reverend Ivor Emmanuel'.

Realising they were genuine he once again apologised and poured them their drinks. The two sat down at a table, Dai smiling to the Reverend,

"We should try this more often! Free drinks are the best drinks I always say."

"Well I know one pub where it would not work," replied the Reverend. "The landlord's a right miserable person."

"What pub's that then Rev?"

"The *Dragon and Daff* in Aberglas," replied the Reverend, raising his glass. Dai laughed.

"Done me like a kipper then! But I have heard the landlady is a lot worse!" and then also raised his glass.

An hour later, and after another round of drinks which this time Dai did have to pay for - much to his disgust - they headed back to the Passport Office. Mrs Morgan Morgan still assumed the same pose.

"How was the church?" she asked the pair of them.

"Most refreshing," smiled Dai.

As they went to sit down Mrs Morgan Morgan's name was called from behind the cubicle. She stood up and entered. Two minutes later she walked out.

"We can leave now," she declared.

"Did you not have it then?" asked Dai.

"Yes, it's in my handbag."

"Give us a look. They are really funny. Look, you show me yours and I will show you mine!"

"Don't be so childish! We have more important things to do. Now let's get back to Brynlog."

The night before they were due to leave for Brussels Dai and Megan held a leaving party at their pub: "Any excuse for a party," laughed Dai.

The Reverend and Mrs Morgan Morgan declined in preference for an early night given their 7am departure for the airport's midday flight. They wanted be fully rested and arrive in plenty of time.

The *Dragon and Daff* was packed with everyone wishing Dai the best of luck and giving him advice on what not to do: "Don't drink the water. It gives you a bad stomach. I had it in India once and I was on the toilet for days," he was told.

Megan laughed: "It's the home of Stella Artois so I don't think he's going to be drinking water!"

"It's not a jolly up," protested Dai, it's an official visit mun!"

But it fell on deaf ears.

Other advice included the purchase of travel insurance, memorising the numbers of the emergency services - and also finding a solicitor.

"I'm going to Brussels, not the Middle East," he exclaimed.

Sian the Shop approached Dai with a going-away present: *The mini-guide to Brussels*. She had highlighted some useful phrases on the last two pages of the book, including: 'Can you tell me where the bar is?' Dai burst out laughing so loud that the whole pub stopped talking. They too then fell about laughing when he told them why. Sian was slightly embarrassed but also privately delighted that everyone had found her joke funny.

As the clock approached 11.20pm Dai thanked the last couple for attending the party. He closed the door behind them and locked up.

"How about it tonight, love? I'm away in the morning to a foreign land."

"As you said love, it's not the Middle East and anyway I have nearly finished my book and I'm taking it back to the library tomorrow. Otherwise my love, if you were going to the Middle East and I had finished my book it would have been your lucky night. But I still love you though and if you're staying up a bit longer, don't wake me up when you come to bed. But if I'm awake you won't have to worry about waking me up. Night love."

She went upstairs. Dai just stood there trying to figure out what Megan's was saying but gave up, walked around the bar and poured himself a large vodka and coke instead. He then settled down with the sports section of the daily paper

The morning of the trip arrived. Dead on 7am Colin the Cabbie pulled up outside the *Dragon and Daff*. He beeped his horn at which Dai exited his premises carrying a sports bag. He opened the boot, put his bag in and got in the back seat next to the Reverend. Mrs Morgan Morgan assumed the front passenger seat.

"Morning all," greeted Dai. Then in his best Winston Churchill voice proclaimed, "We will fight them on the beaches."

"That was nothing like Winny Churchill," laughed the Reverend. "More Winny Mandela!"

"David the Public House. Aren't you forgetting your suitcase? You only put a little bag in the boot."

"That is my luggage," replied Dai. "We are only going overnight. My suit is in there, my two ties, my Sunday shoes, fresh pants and socks."

Mrs Morgan Morgan tutted: "You did not need to give all the details of your attire - especially your unmentionables."

Dai smiled at the Reverend. ""Well in that case I will not mention my unmentionables again!"
As always he laughed at his own joke.

The journey to the airport took just over two hours. After 9am the cab pulled up outside Cardiff International airport departures. Colin helped them extract their luggage and the Reverend paid him the £30 fare they had agreed. The Reverend had promised that if Colin charged him more than £30 he would then 'burn in Hell'. The Reverend really knew how to win an argument.

Dai chucked his bag over his shoulder and went through the doors leaving the other two to drag their own suitcases in. The Reverend had a battered brown leather suitcase with string tied around it that he must have taken off one of the poor war refugees who had been shipped to Aberglas. Mrs Morgan Morgan's luggage was jet black, matching her travelling outfit. Then again, her travelling outfit was the same as her everyday outfit.

They entered Departures, booked in and went for a cup of tea. Dai then espied the 'Fly Us' check-in desk at the very end of the terminal.

Upon arrival they were greeted with a smile by 'Trudy'. Mrs Morgan Morgan immediately barged in front.

"Hello. I'm Mrs Morgan Morgan. Can you call the pilot please as I have some questions about our flight?"

"I am sure I can help you with any of your enquiries," replied Trudy.

"So tell me, young lady, do you fly the plane as well as booking us in? I don't think so. Now can you call the pilot please?"

Trudy picked up the phone: "One moment please."

After a brief discussion she replaced the receiver.

"Whilst you're waiting, can I check you in please?"

"Not until after I have spoken to the pilot," insisted Mrs Morgan Morgan.

At this point the Reverend intervened.

"Hello. You may proceed with my check-in, young lady, if you wish?"

"With pleasure," replied a relieved Trudy, following it with the usual questions - all of which were answered in tones markedly different from the ones he had adopted with Colin during discussion of the taxi fare.

It was then Dai's turn. He stepped up to the counter with a wicked look in his eye.

"The name's 'Dai', love. How are you at this time of the morning? You should still be in bed getting your beauty sleep - but then again, you don't need much, do you?"

Dai always liked to flirt with younger ladies to see if he could still charm them. He should have stopped there and then to answer similar security questions but that was not in Dai's nature.

Trudy started to enter Dai's details. Without looking up from her screen, she asked:

"Did you pack the bag yourself sir?"

"Of course, love. I'm not going to ask the wife to do it. She would get it wrong."

Trudy looked up. Question Two.

"Have you left your bag unattended at anytime?"

"Of course, love. It's been up the attic for over a year. I'm not going to sit up there with it, am I?"

Trudy shook her head. "No, sir. I meant since you got here at the airport?"

"You must be joking! There's a lot of weird people around here," nodding towards Mrs Morgan Morgan.

Trudy smiled and continued.

"Do you have anything sharp in your bag?"

Dai thought for a moment.

"I got a bag of bitter lemons in it. Does that count?"

Trudy strained a grin.

"So that's a 'No' then, and finally has anyone asked you to carry anything through for them this morning?"

"If they did," he laughed, "I would tell them to carry their own stuff through. Lazy buggers."

Trudy handed Dai back his passport with the boarding card inside.

"There we go. Enjoy your flight."

All of a sudden a man in a suit approached Mrs Morgan Morgan.

"Hello. I'm Stuart. I'm the duty manager this morning. How may I help you?"

Mrs Morgan Morgan looked Stuart up and down.

"I said I wished to speak to the pilot. Honestly, how difficult is it to talk to the man?!"

"Well at the moment it is very difficult as he is about an hour away and about 25,000 feet up in the air. He is flying in from Geneva. Then later on he will be taking you to your destination, Brussels, this morning. May I also say I have known the Cptain personally for over ten years so I can answer any queries you may have. May I just ask though, are you a nervous flyer? We do sell some over-the-counter tablets at our Pharmacy, and also you're a lot safer in a plane than you are in a car these days."

"Unless another plane goes through a red cloud. Then we are knacked," quipped Dai.

Mrs Morgan Morgan gave Dai one of her legendary stares, obliging Dai to seek sanctuary behind the Reverend.

However, Dai was six foot two whilst the Reverend was only five foot six, so Mrs Morgan could still see him.

Mrs Morgan Morgan turned away to look back at Stuart.

"I can assure you young man. I never have nor ever will be nervous of anything. Now my questions are, firstly, what are the choices of meal onboard our flight as I refuse to eat anything that is microwaved and served with plastic crockery?"

Stuart went to answer but Mrs Morgan Morgan put up her hand up to stop him.

"You will wait until I have finished all my questions before I allow you to answer. Secondly, I know there is no First Class on the plane but I am requesting a seat at the front so I can keep an eye on the pilot and where we are going. My third question to you is, how long has he been flying? I don't want someone who has just passed his test! And lastly, the in-flight movie: please ensure it's not some violent or sloppy film. Can I request a musical something like *The Sound of Music* or the original *Phantom of the Opera* - not the remake! They ruined it Now, young man, you have my permission to answer."

Stuart stood there for a moment nonplussed. He quickly regained his wits to reply.

"The answer to your first question about the meal is: you may purchase snacks and beverages of your choice from the onboard duty-free service which will move through the cabin during your flight as there is no actual meal served on this flight. The flight is only 2 hours and 50 minutes. In answer to your second question, we at Fly Us airlines operate a non-allocation of seats. Basically you can sit where you want unless you are disabled or have trouble walking. In these cases we normally keep the front seats free. Also even if you sit in the front seats you will not be able to see straight ahead as due to security reasons the deck is locked for the duration of the flight.

"I believe the third question you asked, the length of time the Captain has been flying? Well, he has over 30,000 flying hours under his belt so I can assure you he is one of the most experienced captains. Lastly, there are no in-flight movies but I'm sure you can find and buy some reading material for the flight. Now, if that's all may I wish you a safe flight and assure you that Captain Jones will make your journey as comfortable as possible."

Stuart smiled and started to walk away but Dai called back to him.

"Is Captain Jones Welsh, then?"

"Yes," smiled Stuart. "Born in Cardiff actually."

"Tidy, mun," exclaimed Dai. "If you had said that at the beginning there would not have been any need to question his experience or if he knew where he was going? Everyone knows us Welsh are perfect at everything. Cheers butte."

Dai waved to Stuart who in return threw him a half-hearted smile while walking away as quickly as he could.

Mrs Morgan Morgan returned to the check-in desk and after Trudy had checked her in, the three of them headed to the security scanning checkpoint.

They showed their boarding passes and headed into the main security areas where they were obliged to remove their jackets and shoes, place them in a basket and walk through the metal detector. The Reverend was shocked that Mrs Morgan Morgan did not protest at having to do this. Maybe she was a little nervous of flying but had been reassured by Stuart earlier?

The Reverend passed through the scanner without problem, followed by Mrs Morgan Morgan. Then it came to Dai's turn. As he walked through the scanner, the alarm rang. A guard summoned him to step aside for a pat down.

"Do you have any metal objects still on you, sir?"

Dai shook his head. The guard then worked his way down Dai's body with a portable metal detector. When it reached Dai's waist it beeped manically. Dai was requested to lift up his tee-shirt to reveal the culprit: his belt with the Welsh emblem on it.

"Please remove that sir, and go through the detector again," the guard ordered.

"If I do that, mun, my jeans will be around my ankles!"

"I'm sorry sir. You have to. Otherwise you may not be allowed to travel this morning."

Dai duly unbuckled his belt and made his way back through the metal detector. He then turned around and opened his legs as if he was astride an invisible horse. This time, no alarms rang. The guard handed Dai back his belt and thanked him. Dai started walking away then realised he had not replaced his belt. Quickly, he grabbed his jeans as they started to fall down. He replaced his belt, grabbed his coat, shoes and other items from the basket, and headed over to where the other two were waiting for him.

"Can't you just do anything without causing a scene?" snarled Mrs Morgan Morgan at Dai.

The Reverend looked at Dai in disbelief.

"Excuse me. Which one of us has just spent the last 20 minutes downstairs finding out everything about our flight and the driver of our plane? The only thing you did not ask was what he had for breakfast!"

"My questions were valid as they weren't just for me but for every other passenger travelling with us today. And I did not just make a scene in front of everyone at the airport by not following the correct procedure. Some people just don't know how to act properly in public."

With that she headed off for some reading material. Dai and the Reverend just looked at each other, shook their heads and followed on behind her.

Mrs Morgan Morgan made her way to the newspaper shop. There was no way she was going to be forced to talk to those two for the full flight. Dai and the Reverend meanwhile went to one of the bars for some light refreshments.

The two of them sat there discussing what they were going to say to the Human Rights Court when Mrs Morgan Morgan re-appeared with a book in hand. She informed them that years ago her purchase would have been wrapped in a plastic bag but that now "they are trying to charge me five pence for one and I'm only advertising the firm that is trying to charge me. Now everyone will see what reading matter I have!"

The Reverend looked at the book: *The Merry Widow* - a story about a woman who got away with murdering her husband. He glanced at Dai. Mrs Morgan Morgan stood up.

"Well, I'm going to the ladies' bathroom but it's OK, I will get my own cup of tea when I return."

Dai smiled. "It's OK. I will get it for you. It will be my pleasure."

Dai could also get another lager for himself.

Mrs Morgan Morgan left her book face up on the table. The Reverend considered its title:

"Nice happy book for a flight."

"It's most properly homework - or a checklist," he spluttered.

Eventually they were called to board their flight.

"I have just realised that we don't have an appointment," exclaimed the Reverend suddenly. "I hope they let us in."

"Do you know it takes a woman to do a man's job? I phoned two days ago and we have a two o'clock meeting tomorrow with a Mr..." she then opened her handbag retrieving a piece of paper with the name, "...a Mr Philipe Lyon. Honestly, I don't know how men survive in this world!"

Dai bit his tongue. He was itching to say, 'Well, three of your husbands didn't survive!' but instead sipped his lager.

Chapter Five

The invasion of Belgium

"All passengers for flight FU266 to Brussels: your flight is now boarding at Gate Eight. Can all passengers please make their way there?"

The three of them had already been sitting by Gate Eight for half an hour as Mrs Morgan Morgan wanted to ensure that they would be the first passengers on the plane. As they arose, the queue behind them began to grow. When an airport worker passed behind them, pushing an old lady in a wheelchair up to the front followed by an elderly man and a younger woman, Mrs Morgan Morgan felt bound to speak.

"Excuse me. There's a queue here. We have been standing here for 32 minutes."

The airport worker looked at her in disbelief.

"This lady has priority boarding due to her walking difficulties."

"Well, the other two have no problem walking, so they can go to the back of the queue!" she exclaimed, pointing at her companions.

The Fly Us employee behind the desk ready to take the tickets and check boarding passes, intervened.

"Excuse me but it's our policy to board passengers that need special assistance first. And surely you are not going to complain that her husband and granddaughter are also going with her? I must ask, how would you like it if the two gentlemen you're travelling with were not sitting by you?"

"If you could possibly do that, I would be very grateful," smiled Mrs Morgan Morgan.

The last of the passengers settled. Mrs Morgan Morgan, the Reverend and Dai occupied the front row opposite the passengers who had been boarded first. Mrs Morgan Morgan still had her handbag on her lap and whilst the air hostess was checking the seatbelts she noticed Mrs Morgan Morgan.

"Excuse me, madam. All hand luggage must be stowed in the overhead locker for the duration of the flight."

"First of all, miss, I'm not a 'madam'. I'm Mrs Morgan Morgan. Also this is not hand luggage: it's a handbag. Can't you tell the difference? I thought they would have taught you that before you were allowed to become air staff. Honestly, these days as long as you fit the uniform they give you a job. In my days you had to train for many years to get a promotion but these days they just promote willy nilly. No wonder the country's in the state it's in."

The air hostess stood her ground.

"I will have you know I trained for over two years to get to this position and I know it's a handbag but it must be stowed in the overhead locker. It's for your safety as well as your fellow passengers and unless you let me stow it you will be removed from this flight. It's your choice."

"Why, you should have said it was for safety reasons," exclaimed a mollified Mrs Morgan Morgan. Of course you may stow it. You should have explained yourself a bit better young lady."

In her mind she had once again won the battle, this time by stating that the air hostess had not explained herself properly – despite having to give up her handbag.

The Captain announced that there would then follow a safety demonstration: "and we ask all passengers, even frequent flyers, to pay close attention."

The engines started as the air hostesses commenced the demonstration, and the plane began to reverse.

"I can't keep my handbag on my lap," said Mrs Morgan Morgan to the Reverend, "but they are allowed to stand up as the plane is taking off! Well, it will be their own fault if they hurt themselves. And I'm not going to administer first aid if they do."

"We have not taken off yet. The pilot's just lining up the plane ready."

The engines roared into life, the plane started to shudder and then the brakes were released. The craft then charged down the runway at speed. The Reverend and Dai closed their eyes and gripped onto the armrests. Mrs Morgan Morgan meanwhile looked out of the window in awe as the plane left the ground. She appeared amazed as the ground faded away, replaced by blue sky as it made its way through the clouds. Jolting slightly, the aircraft levelled out and the hostesses released their seatbelts. They started to move around the cabin. Another announcement followed.

"I'm Tina. I'm your head flight crew member for this flight. Today with me are Julie and Gina. The seatbelt sign is still on so please remain seated until the Captain turns it off. And when sitting in your seat we advise you to keep your seatbelt on in case of any unexpected turbulence."

Mrs Morgan Morgan looked over at the Reverend, now himself staring out of the window. Dai still had his eyes closed. His knuckles remained white as he was still gripping the armrest. The Reverend tapped Dai on the shoulder.

"Are you all right, Dai? You don't look very well."

Dai opened his eyes. "I'm fine, mun. I'm not scared of flying. I'm not scared of anything! Worked down the mines I did!"

Dai privately wished that he was still underground or at least on the ground but he was not going to show them that he was actually petrified. He glimpsed at his watch: two hours and 35 minutes left. He would rather face Megan in a bad mood than go through this, he thought to himself.

The Captain shortly made the sort of announcement that everyone dreads:

"Ladies and Gentleman. Please return to your seats immediately as we are about to go through a bit of bad weather which might cause some turbulence. We will try and go through it as gently as possible."

The whole plane fell silent. People sat back in their seats. Then the plane started shuddering violently. Dai grabbed the Reverend's hand. The Reverend did not seem to notice as he had his eyes closed and was no doubt praying to his superior. After about five minutes - which seemed more like five hours - the plane settled once more, and the seatbelt light disappeared.

Dai rushed to the toilet at the back of the plane. He shortly returned with a bit more colour in his cheeks.

"You all right Dai?" enquired the Reverend.

"Yes, I wasn't sick - just needed to go to the toilet."

"I didn't say, 'Had you vomited?' I just asked if you were OK? Don't be so paranoid!"

"I'm just saying. That's all," replied Dai trying to remove the current taste from his mouth with a mint he had found in his pocket earlier.

Ten minutes later, Dai stood up again.

"Right. I need to go again now."

The Reverend looked at Mrs Morgan Morgan. "I think our Dai does not like flying."

"He is not *our* Dai. He might be *yours* but he is certainly not *mine*. I don't see what his problem is. This is great - and you should be happy too. You're closer to your boss than you have ever been. Up here you can see for miles. I can see fields down there and also another plane over there," she exclaimed pointing.

"He's a bit close! Hope he can see us!"

In fact the other plane was 20 miles away and 10,000 feet above them but as it was so clear up there it looked closer than it was.

Dai returned to his seat: "That should do the trick!"

"Dai. Why do you keep using the toilet down the other end of the plane when there's one just by there?" he asked, pointing to the door with 'WC' above it.

"That's no good. I can't advertise if I use that one." The Reverend looked puzzled. Dai pointed to his tee-shirt. On the front of it was printed *Dragon and Daff Public House*. Dai then turned around to show him the back: 'Phone Aberglas on 00184 754344. Open seven days a week'.

"You can't fault having a captive audience. It's also the best price for advertising as it's free!" he winked.

They were about an hour into the flight when the plane started shuddering again. Dai pressed the call button above his head and shortly Gina turned up.

"Can I help you sir?"

"Are we going through more turbulence at the moment?"

"No sir," smiled Gina.

"Well in that case, ask the driver to slow down. Doesn't he know it's bumpy back here, mun? Tell him it's not how fast you get there, it's just getting there that counts."

The rest of the flight passed off calmly – which Dai attributed to the fact that the pilot had taken his advice.

They soon landed at Brussels and the plane taxied to the gate. Upon disembarkation they would pass Captain Jones and his co-pilot as they had left the flight deck to wish everyone a farewell.

"Glad to see you took my advice, butte," beamed Dai to Captain Jones. "You are never too old to learn," he declared, slapping him on the shoulder.

The Captain looked puzzled as he passed. Gina laughed, and after the last passenger had exited, explained precisely what Dai had meant.

"If you see him on one of our flights again, please let me know so that he can fly the plane instead of me. It would be nice to be a passenger for a change!"

All the crew burst out laughing.

Mrs Morgan Morgan, the Reverend and Dai stood with the other passengers at the luggage carousel. Finally the three of them claimed their belongings and headed out through the Arrivals door. Mrs Morgan Morgan scanned the people standing there with name cards. None bore her's.

"I told him to send a car. You wait till I see them in the morning. I will give him such a piece of my mind and before you say it, David the Public House, yes I can afford to give him a piece."

"I would never say that," and then thought to himself, 'Damn. It would have been funny if I had said it'.

Anyway, they decided not to wait any longer for the Diplomatic Car and headed out instead for a taxi to the hotel.

Before the driver moved off, Mrs Morgan Morgan informed him plainly that she had a map so that he would not try to bump up the price by taking the long way around. Shortly, the taxi driver indicated his intention to turn left down the N2.

"You're not supposed to go down here. You can stay on this road to get to the hotel."

The taxi driver tried to explain that there were roadworks on the other road.

"It does not show any roadworks on this map! Are you sure you're not taking us the long way round?"

"If you're unhappy with my driving I will let you get off here, particularly if you think you know this place better than me, who was born here and have driven taxis for 20 years."

The Reverend tapped Mrs Morgan Morgan on the shoulder.

"Let him just get us to the hotel. I'm sure he is not trying to exploit us. I'm sure he is just trying to get us to the hotel as quickly as he can."

This seemed to calm the driver but put Mrs Morgan Morgan in a bad mood. The remainder of the journey passed in silence.

Finally the taxi pulled up outside the hotel. The Reverend paid the fare and asked for a receipt explaining they were on an official visit and needed it for tax purposes. In other words, he was making sure that if anyone at home queried any of the money spent he could prove everything to them. But if they did dare ask he would condemn them all to eternal Hell for questioning his honesty.

They checked in and went to their rooms. The Reverend unpacked his luggage, carefully placing everything on individual hangers. Dai, on the other hand, opened his bag and placed all his clothes in neat piles on the floor.

"Right then, Rev. Time to sample the local cuisine. You up for it?"

"Actually I am a bit peckish. Yes, I might have something to eat as well. So what local cuisine did you mean?"

"Stella Artois, mun. It's local. Shall we knock the Dragon's door on our way to see if she wants to join us or shall we just sneak past?"

"We can't just sneak out and leave her alone. It's unchristian."

"You're right. You go and ask her and I will meet you in the bar just in case she decides to come with us. I'm going to need some anaesthetic to numb the pain."

Dai decided to sit by the empty bar's window and watch the world go by. He was soon joined by the Reverend.

"I have some bad news for you Dai. Mrs Morgan Morgan has a bit of a headache so has decided to lie down for an hour."

"Well in that case another pint is called for to celebrate. You up for one, Rev?"

"Well, when in Rome."

"We are in Brussels, mun, not Rome."

The Reverend shook his head in disbelief. "Never mind. I will have a small wine thanks."

Dai went up to the bar.

"Another pint butte, and a large wine."

The barman looked at him. "

"Just a large wine then?"

Dai shook his head: "…and a pint, butte."

"But what?" asked the barman looking very confused. Dai laughed. "No mun. You know 'butte'? 'Butte'? You understand me?"

Now this confused the barman even more.

"OK. Let's start again. Same for me and also a large wine for my Father."

Dai returned with the drinks.

"I said 'a small one'."

"Well, when in Rome drink like you're in Brussels." With that he raised his glass: "Cheers Rev."

Joining in, the Reverend then invited Dai to join him sightseeing: "We are not going to have much time tomorrow and it would be a pity to come all this way just to sit in the hotel bar."

To the Reverend's amazement Dai agreed.

"I don't want to spend all afternoon in the hotel bar either. There must be other bars we can see."

"Dai. Sometimes you're incorrigible."

"Nah, I'm a Taurus, mun."

Both laughed.

With help from a free map from the hotel reception, they headed out to explore the city of Brussels. First on the agenda was the 'Manneken Pis'. The Reverend informed Dai that it was built between 1617 and 1619, had survived the bombardment of Brussels and donned over 700 suits which are changed several times a week."

Dai looked confused.

"He's a statue and has over several hundred suits? I'm a human and only got the one: a black one and it's used for funerals and weddings, and if I knew anybody Jewish I would use it also for a bar mitzvah. These Belgiums must have some short people to have had so many hand-me-downs!"

When they arrived at the statue the Reverend told Dai that it was used many centuries ago as the main source of drinking water. Dai looked at its water flowing out of the little boy's penis.

"They must have been joking if they expected the locals to drink the water from there! No wonder they invented Stella Artois. Talk about taking the pee!"

"Quiet! You don't want to upset the locals. This is very close to their hearts."

"How can I upset the locals, mun? They drink water out of a penis, for goodness sake. And Megan shouts at me if I drink milk from the plastic bottle! I'm going to take a photo of this and next time she shouts at me I am going to show her."

With that he took out his disposable camera for a couple of photos.

"Why did you not fetch your real camera?" asked the Reverend. Frightened it might get damaged?"

"No, but if for some reason I take an unflattering photo or get drunk and Mrs Morgan Morgan tries to drop me in it, I will just chuck this camera in the bin, see?" pointing to his head. "Up here for thinking; down there for dancing, then..." pointing at his crotch redundant in the middle.

"Don't know how Megan puts up with you!"

"She lies back and thinks of Wales," winked Dai.

They stayed there for about twenty minutes after which the Reverend suggested their next tourist attraction: the Cathedral of St Michael's and Saint Gudula. He explained that Saint Gudula was the Patron Saint of Brussels: "It's also the only Cathedral that houses a pair of peregrine falcons."

Proud of his knowledge, the Reverend made for the attraction. Dai walked behind, mumbling to himself that he would rather go to Marks and Spencer with Megan than do this. At least the St Michael's in Brynlog had a pub close to it.

The pair decided to catch a tram to the Cathedral. The STIB transport system was known for its simplicity, and after their visit to the Cathedral even Dai was amazed at how lovely it was.

By 5pm the pair of them were back in the hotel bar having concluded their tour with Little Europe.

"I wonder if Mrs Morgan Morgan has woken from the Dragon's den yet?

"I will go and check to see if she is well enough to join us for some dinner," replied the Reverend. "Then I think I will have a shower and some quiet time to myself before this evening, if that's OK with you, Dai?"

"Carry on, mun. I will stay here to reflect on the wonders of Brussels."

"You mean you're going to have another pint?"

"Wow! You can read me better than you can read the Bible."

The Reverend left and headed to Mrs Morgan Morgan's room. The big clock behind the bar chimed six o'clock. Dai supped the last dregs from his glass and returned it to the bar.

"Cheers mate. Don't call last orders till I'm back."

The barman smiled.

"Monsieur, the bar does not close till 1am for guests so we will be open for your return I assure you."

"Magic. Love this place. You're a legend you know."

Despite not fully understanding Dai's accent the barman smiled and put his thumbs up too: "OK, magic."

Dai laughed out loud and headed for his room. Knocking on the door, in his best French accent he shouted,

"Security! Do you have a woman in there?"

The door opened. The Reverend had a shocked look on his face but before he could say anything Dai shouted,

"If you don't have one, would you like a woman for your room?"

He then tapped the Reverend on the shoulder as he entered.

"You should have seen your face, mun! Priceless, it was. Did you get a response from the black widow?"

"Mrs Morgan Morgan is feeling a lot better and will meet us at reception at 8pm this evening."

"Well, in that case I'm going to get my head down for an hour, then have a quick shower and a shave - and I'm all yours."

Dai clambered to his bed. Within five minutes he was snoring his head off. The Reverend had already changed into his dark blue suit and realised that he was not going to have any peace to read his Bible. He therefore decided to go down to the reading lounge he had seen it on the way up: nice big leather armchairs and no television. He left Dai a note to say he would also meet him at the hotel reception at eight.

They had booked a table in the restaurant for 8.30. At just past 8pm the lift door opened and out stepped Dai wearing a black pair of trousers, black shoes and a tee-shirt with his pub name written across it; 'Thirsty and Welsh' adorned the back. He spotted the other two on the plush leather armchairs in the hotel foyer.

Mrs Morgan Morgan took a deep breath.

"David the Public House. This is not a rugby tour. This is an official visit. Please go back upstairs to your room and find more suitable attire. If you think I'm going to have a meal with someone who looks like they have just got dressed in a power cut, you're very much mistaken."

The Reverend shook his head as Dai looked for some moral support. Dai then saw that the Reverend was wearing a suit and tie and that Mrs Morgan Morgan had an even more formal black dress on than usual. She had also removed her hat.

"I only brought one clean shirt, mun."

"Well in that case you had better make sure you don't get any stains on it at dinner. You will be needing it tomorrow."

Dai knew he was beaten so went back to change.

Before getting in the lift he shouted,

"Your round, Rev. Mine's a Stella. Won't be long!"

Returning shortly, Dai joined his companions. The waiter from the restaurant entered the hotel bar and walked up to where the three of them sat. Dai was now in his only suit, white shirt and blue tie.

"Excuse me. Your table is now ready if you would like to follow me please."

"Good!" announced Dai rubbing his hands together. "I'm staving. Could eat a scabby horse."

Mrs Morgan Morgan and the Reverend cringed.

"Don't think that's on the menu tonight," quipped the Reverend.

The restaurant was, in Dai's words, "a bit posh for some nosh". They were escorted to their table.

"Hope they do proper food. Don't want any of that new cuisine stuff."

The Reverend smiled. "It's not 'new cuisine', Dai. It's 'nouvelle cuisine'."

"Well, I don't want any of that stuff either."

Dai beckoned the waiter over.

"Excuse me, butte. Can you grab us a Stella and..." pointing to the Reverend, "You up for a wine?"

The Reverend nodded. "I would not normally but just this once."

Dai looked at him: 'Just this once,' he thought. 'You have had a lot of 'once's' since we have been here,' "and for you..." pointing at Mrs Morgan Morgan,

"A glass of water, please."

"Oh come. Have a proper drink for once."

Mrs Morgan Morgan took a deep breath:

"Very well. Double gin and tonic on the rocks with a twist please."

Dai's mouth fell open in shock.

"Go girl. That's the spirit - or a double spirit even!"

Mrs Morgan Morgan smiled.

"David the Public House. Just because I'm not in your public house every night does not mean that I don't like a drink. So close your mouth please before you start catching flies."

The waiter returned with their drinks while they perused the menu.

"They got horses duvets. Must be for someone on a stable diet!"

Once again he laughed at his own joke louder than the other two.

The waiter placed the drinks down.

"I will give you some more time before I take your order," he smiled.

Mrs Morgan Morgan looked at Dai.

"Congratulations on embarrassing all of us. It's not horses duvets, it's hors d'oeuvre. It's an appetiser. Have you never been to a nice restaurant before?"

"How dare you! I took Megan to a really fancy restaurant once in Cardiff. We were still in Wales but at least the menu was in English. Why is this menu in a foreign language here?"

"Maybe because we are in Belgium," stated the Reverend.

"That's beside the point. It should have it in English as well."

"Gentlemen. Calm yourself Reverend Emmanuel. You are a man of the cloth. Just because you have a wine does not mean you can act like some sort of lout. Also, David the Public House, turn the menu to page four: the menu there is in English."

"Oh good."

Quick as a flash he closed the menu and said,

"I will have the soup."

"For the main course?"

"No, I want the soup for starters," declard Dai.

Mrs Morgan Morgan started to get annoyed. The Reverend noticed and tapped her hand.

"Mrs Morgan Morgan meant what are you going to have for the main course?"

Dai picked up the menu again and without opening it declared,

"I'm going to have the rump steak well done with chips and fresh vegetables."

He replaced the menu. The Reverend looked amazed.

"How do you know that they have steak with vegetables on the menu without even looking at the main courses?"

"When you went up for a shower earlier I noticed the bar menu. I asked the barman if he had the restaurant menu as well and decided there and then what I was going to have before I came upstairs."

This time it was Mrs Morgan Morgan's turn to calm the Reverend down.

"Oh come on. I was only having a laugh, mun. Don't be so serious all the time. It's like being at a wake with you two. We will have plenty of time to be serious tomorrow when we take on the world."

This finally brought a smile to the other two.

The Reverend decided on melon as a starter and trout for the main course. Mrs Morgan Morgan went for pâté but could not decide on the main course.

"I want something that comes with a sauce but is not too strong."

Dai perused his menu.

"Why don't you have a Steak Diane?"

Mrs Morgan Morgan looked straight back at Dai:

""Who told you?! Tell me! Who told you?"

Dai became scared and puzzled at the same time. He moved his chair back.

"Told me what?"

"Who told you that my christian name was Diane? Did you look at my passport when I checked in? That's an invasion of privacy! I could have you arrested for that."

Dai's expression immediately betrayed to Mrs Morgan Morgan that it was just a lucky guess.

"No! What I meant was, why don't you have the Steak Diane? It comes with a sauce. Steak Diane it is then."

The poor Reverend has just taken a sip of his wine and nearly choked.

"Take your time, Rev. Don't want you to die in front of Di and Dai, do we Di?"

Mrs Morgan Morgan glared at Dai.

"Look, David the Public House. Let me tell you now that if anyone finds out my name I will know where it came from and I will make your life hell. Do you understand?"

"Too late," retorted Dai. "I'm already married and looking forward to dying and living in Hell. Bet it's nicer there - and with a bit of luck the Rev by here will have a word with him upstairs and let Megan into Heaven. At least then I've only got the Devil to deal with."

The Reverend smiled: "I will see what I can do."

Mrs Morgan Morgan pointed at Dai:

"I mean it! I know that the Reverend will take the secret of my name to the grave, so there will only be one culprit and one victim if people find out my name."

The waiter returned to take the Reverend's and Dai's orders. Then it was Mrs Morgan Morgan's turn. She requested the paté first ...followed by a Steak Diane. The other two could not contain their laughter while the waiter simply appeared puzzled: why this was so funny and why did Mrs Morgan Morgan still sit there with a straight face? Dai looked at the waiter, tears running down his face.

"You had to be there, mun!"

The waiter merely smiled, nodded and beat a hasty retreat.

The meal itself was thoroughly enjoyable and for a change the three of them engaged in a normal conversation ranging from the state of the world, to the lovely sites the Reverend and Dai had seen on their visit of Brussels earlier. They told Mrs Morgan Morgan that if they had time tomorrow they would take her to the Cathedral so that she could see it for herself.

They then returned to the bar. It was the busiest Dai had seen it since their arrival but they still managed to sit at his - now regular - table. The Reverend bought the drinks and Mrs Morgan Morgan took out from her handbag the list of questions they were going to ask Mr Lyon in the morning.

"Where are the signed petitions?" she asked Dai.

"Never fear, Dai's here," he smiled. "They are safe and sound in my bag upstairs."

"Do you know how many signatures we got in the end?" enquired the Reverend, causing Dai to ponder for a few seconds.

"721."

"That's absolutely great! What a fantastic result for us," exclaimed the Reverend.

"Well, I just hope that this Mr Lyon is not a sports fan" replied Dai.

"What do you mean, a sports fan?" queried Mrs Morgan Morgan.

"Well, let's put it another way. We were a bit short of names so I kind of added some names of people that I didn't ask."

The Reverend closed his eyes.

"OK Dai. Whose name did you sign without asking them first?"

"Well, I might have slightly forged the names of the 1980s' British and Irish Lions. Also Mervin Davies - known as merv the swerve - J P R Williams ... well, actually most of the Welsh internationals of the 70s and also the Swansea City team who played in Europe. But don't worry. They did not play in this country so I think we are safe. Also I might have added some of the characters from some of my favourite films."

"Well," sighed the Reverend, "you are going to get your wish of going to Hell anyway. What happens if he looks through them and sees, I don't know, Rocky Balboa?"

"Damn. Forgot that one!" joked Dai. "But you don't really think he is going to sit there and go through every name, do you? Most probably as soon as we leave he will call his secretary and tell her to file the petition under 'S'. You know…'S' for 'Shredder'. We are not important enough to have someone actually take the time to check that all the names are correct. It's sorted."

"Well," rebuffed Mrs Morgan Morgan, "we may not be that important but I assure you that after tomorrow we will never be forgotten! Now let's go through the questions."

Mrs Morgan Morgan started with Question One. The clock behind the bar chimed. Dai glanced up at it and then back at his watch in case it was wrong.

"Wow!" It's midnight. A quick one for the road then I'm off to bed. You two up for a nightcap?"

To Dai's surprise they both answered in the affirmative.

"I'm in shock! I did not realise you two were such a pair of alcoholics!"

A few minutes later Dai returned with a large wine, a double gin and tonic, one pint of Stella and a big brandy.

"Who's the brandy for?" enquired the Reverend.

"That's my nightcap," replied Dai.

"So who's the lager for then?" asked Mrs Morgan Morgan.

"That's my pre-nightcap."

By 12.45am the three of them were fast asleep, Dai and the Reverend having a snoring contest in their room. Luckily, next door was unoccupied; luckier still was the fact that Mrs Morgan Morgan's room was further down the corridor. She was a light sleeper and would never have had any rest if she was in a 20-yard radius of them.

Chapter Six

Part Two

The alarm rang at 8am. Dai tried to switch it off but merely ended up smacking his hand on the bedroom cabinet. He opened his eyes only to be greeted by the sight of the Reverend standing there with the alarm clock in his hand.

"Good morning Dai. It's time to get up. You're lucky I let you sleep in 'til this time as I was thinking of calling you at 6.30 when I woke up. I don't know how you can sleep so late! I have already been out for a walk to blow the cobwebs away. So come on: rise and shine!"

"OK, I'm awake!" groaned Dai. "Have you got any aspirins?"

The Reverend smiled.

"Sorry. Never use tablets. I believe the pain will go away through the power of prayer. Mrs Morgan Morgan might have some. Why don't you ask her when we get downstairs?"

The lift door opened to reveal Mrs Morgan Morgan sitting on the leather chair in Reception.

"Good afternoon gentlemen."

The Reverend smiled, explaining that he had woken up early and already been for a morning stroll; Dai merely proffered a feeble smile.

"I need a coffee."

"David the Public House! You look like death. I have laid out dead people that looked better than you do this morning. Do you have a hangover by any chance?"

Dai once again gave a half-hearted smile.

"Don't suffer from hangovers. I think I got jetlag."

"You can't have jetlag!" laughed the Reverend. "We were only in the air for just over two hours. To suffer from jetlag you need to fly to somewhere a lot further that also has a different time zone!"

Dai looked at his watch.

"What time is it in Aberglas, Rev?"

"It's an hour behind: five to eight."

"What's the time here at the moment?"

"Five to nine."

Dai folded his arms: "See, there's a different time zone between here and Aberglas so, as I said, I must be suffering from jetlag."

The Reverend shook his head.

"Nice try."

Dai shifted his attention to Mrs Morgan Morgan.

"Do you have some aspirins by any chance?"

"What do you think I am? A retired matron of 37 years: do you think I would not come prepared?"

"In that case, may I please have a couple of aspirins?"

Mrs Morgan Morgan searched for them in her handbag.

"Sorry, David the Public House. I forgot to bring them."

The bar's clock chimed nine. To Dai it was as if Big Ben was ringing inside his head. He tried standing up but almost fell back down again.

"Right. You two stay here. Me go to Pharmacy."

His head was so bad that he could not even string a proper sentence together. Dai begged the Receptionist to tell him where the nearest Chemist's was located. Luckily, it was just around the corner.

Dai picked up the first packet of aspirins he could find and ripped it open. He stuck four of them in his mouth, crushing them with his teeth before trying to swallow them. He started to choke on the powdery residue but then saw a bottle of water on the shelf. Twisting the cap as hard as he could, he poured the refreshing liquid down his throat and staggered to the checkout.

"Just these please, love. Don't bother with a bag."

Dai returned to the hotel. He was still rather wobbly on his feet, incurring censure from Mrs Morgan Morgan.

"Do you realise, David the Public House, that you are not only showing yourself up being in this state but also the British in general?"

"Excuse me Diane but I'm not British: I'm Welsh - and to be a proper Welshman you have to prove your drinking capabilities even if it means that you pray for death the following day. And anyway, I repeat I am *not* hungover. I am suffering from jetlag."

"I'm a Welshman, Dai, but I'm not praying for death this morning," retorted the Reverend.

Dai scowled.

"You pray for everything everyday. I'm sure that once you must have made a mistake and prayed to die."

The Reverend looked skywards.

"Well, the closest I have ever come to praying for death was for a certain referee in charge of the rugby international between England and Wales, when we were robbed and England cheated and won. But I meant no harm to him."

"How can you pray for the referee to die and mean no harm to him? You men make no sense whatsoever! And don't think I did not notice what you said to me, David the Public House."

"It's too early for riddles. What do you mean, woman?"

Mrs Morgan Morgan lent towards Dai as if she was about to impart something of the utmost confidence.

"The mere fact that you called me 'Diane' might have you wanting to pray for death! Call me that again and your wish will come true. Understand?"

"Stop picking on me! I'm bad. You would not like it if the roles were reversed, would you?"

"The trouble is," interrupted the Reverend, "that Mrs Morgan Morgan and I can hold our drink, butte boy. Now let's stop arguing and go for some breakfast. I'm feeling a bit peckish."

They wandered down the road a few yards when Dai sniffed loudly.

"I can smell bacon."

His companions regarded him dismissively.

"I mean it," he repeated. "I can smell bacon coming from down there."

And off he went.

Amazingly, Dai was right. Fifty yards up the road was the European Café. It advertised its menu in English, French, German and Italian.

"This will do."

And in went Dai, bemusedly followed by the others.

A friendly waitress approached.

"Which language, please?"

"Welsh please love," quipped Dai.

"Sorry, we don't have a Welsh menu. Can you understand an English menu?"

"I will try," he winked.

The Reverend and Mrs Morgan both decided upon a croissant and pot of tea but Dai went for the full breakfast: bacon, sausage, beans, tomatoes, fried bread, fried eggs and toast - with a mug of coffee. Mrs Morgan Morgan looked shocked.

"How come 40 minutes ago you were praying for death and now you are trying to give yourself a heart attack? I think it would have been more sensible if you had decided on a croissant, like the Reverend and myself."

"I was thinking of having the same as you two but the menu advertised the bacon as 'Asda' bacon and sausage - just like at home. Can't fault it."

Twenty minutes later saw Dai supping the last drop of coffee from his mug and smacking his satisified stomach.

"That hit the spot. Filled a tidy hole, that did. Should keep me sorted now 'til dinner!"

"I hope you're not going to throw up as soon as we go outside? That was a lot of grease for someone who is suffering from a hangover!"

"How many times must I tell you? It's not a hangover, it's jetlag, mun."

"It's now 9.55," declared Mrs Morgan Morgan. "You had better go back to the hotel and change, David the Public House. There is no way you're going to meet Mr Lyon dressed like that."

Dai looked down at his polo shirt complete with the *Dragon and Daffodil* badge, and then at his jeans.

"You want me to change my top? It's new! I only got it last year."

The Reverend could see Dai was just trying to wind up Mrs Morgan Morgan.

"Now stop it Dai boy Bach. We have to be united, as one today. Now go back to the hotel and put that suit on that you fetched with you."

"OK. We will call a truce today. Right, sister? I shall return in full battle dress. Remember: we shall bite them on the features and fight them on the beaches also. I will go ahead, scout and then meet you both back at headquarters. Over and out!"

With that he clenched his fist to his mouth and made a noise as if he had switched the mic off. Mrs Morgan Morgan looked at the Reverend.

"Do you think it was a good idea to allow him to come with us? I'm a bit concerned he is not taking this seriously at all."

"I can assure you that despite his jovial appearance Dai is a very proud Welshman - and Aberglassen. He will fight to the last to ensure he gets what's best for him and the village. He also makes me laugh with his sunny disposition - I have even noticed you smiling at him a couple of times as well!"

They both returned to the hotel, shortly to be rejoined by Dai springing out of the lift in his black suit, white shirt and black tie sporting a *Dragon and Daff* logo.

"Well, scrub up well don't I?" he smiled, waiting for their approval.

"Very smart, Dai," agreed the Reverend.

Mrs Morgan Morgan eyes went straight to Dai's tie.

"Haven't you got a plain black tie? I mean, do you have to advertise everywhere you go? I would be very surprised if you did not have the *Dragon and Daffodil* embroidered on your underpants and socks as well!"

"Hang on, I think I have! Do you want a look?"

He approached Mrs Morgan Morgan and grabbed his belt as if he was going to undo it.

"Oh my God!" screamed Mrs Morgan Morgan, raising her handbag over her eyes. Dai laughed so loud that the people in the foyer all stopped to stare at him.

"It's OK folks. Nothing to see here," he laughed, "but plenty to see in there," he roared, tapping his trousers.

Mrs Morgan Morgan was still hiding behind her handbag while begging the Reverend stop Dai making a spectacle of himself. Otherwise he would not be allowed to accompany them to this morning's meeting.

"Now Dai, that's enough! A joke's a joke but you have gone a bit too far now. Act your age please."

"Don't know how to act my age," shrugged Dai. "Never been this age before. And anyway, it was only a bit of fun it was, mun."

"I am going to the ladies' bathroom," suddenly announced Mrs Morgan Morgan standing up. "When I return, we will leave."

"It was only a bit of fun," repeated a crestfallen Dai. "I would not have really stripped in front of her. You know that, don't you?"

"I know you wouldn't have, Dai. But time and a place boy, time and a place. I have to tell you though, you should have seen her face! Can't decide whether it was shock, horror, disgust or panic but it was funny, I must admit. I won't admit it in front of Mrs Morgan Morgan so keep it to yourself, boyo. And anyway I will deny all knowledge of this conversation - and who is she going to believe: you or me? If I was a betting man I would put all my money on me."

Mrs Morgan Morgan returned fully composed.

"Well, gentleman. Shall we go and sort out this silly proposal once and for all? I have just ordered us a taxi. He should be outside."

With that Mrs Morgan Morgan straightened her hat and marched out of the door, dutifully followed by the Reverend and Dai.

The taxi pulled up at the entrance to the visitors' car park, just outside the courts.

"Excuse me," started Mrs Morgan Morgan to the taxi driver. "We are the Welsh delegates. You should have driven us to the front doors."

The taxi driver appeared confused.

"May I enquire then why you asked for a taxi this morning and do not have a diplomatic car fetching you here?"

"It's being washed today, mate," quipped Dai tapping him on the shoulder as they bundled out of the vehicle.

They shortly passed through some very large doors leading to Reception, whereupon a security guard greeted them.

"Good morning. How may I help you?"

"We have an appointment with Mr Phillipe Lyon," declared Mrs Morgan Morgan, speaking for all three of them. "Please inform him we are here."

"May I take your name, please," smiled the guard.

"It's Mrs Morgan Morgan."

"Excuse me? What was your name again?"

"The name is Mrs Morgan Morgan," she repeated.

"Please take a seat. I will inform Mr Lyon of your presence."

Dai picked up an information brochure from the table there. He noticed that it contained not only a map of the building but also a list of the delegates employed there.

"Damn Bach! I don't believe it!"

"What's the matter, Dai?" enquired the Reverend.

"We are in the wrong building!" declared Dai. "Even worse, we are in the wrong country also."

"What you mean, Dai?" replied the Reverend, blankly. "Has your jetlag kicked in again?

"No. Look mun," he insisted as he pointed at the flyer. "The court of Human Rights is in Strasbourg, France, not Brussels in Belgium. We should be over there somewhere…"

The Reverend removed his spectacles from his pocket and regarded the flyer.

"You're right. We are in the wrong building *and* the wrong country! How can we have been so stupid? We are not only going to be the laughing stock of the village but also of Wales!"

Mrs Morgan Morgan did not flinch and merely bided her time in response.

"When you two have quite finished I will calm your fears. We are in the right place and certainly the right country. I know the court of Human Rights is in France but Mr Lyon is here in Brussels. He was the man who helped out that other village your friend David the Inn of Brynlog told us about. So he will know what we can do and help us. Honestly, if I had left it up to you two we would have ended up in France!"

She shook her head in disbelief. Dai mouthed to the Reverend that this was still going to be a waste of time and to leave but once more Mrs Morgan Morgan anticipated his reaction.

"Once again, David the Public House. Stop talking behind my back. Believe me, I know what I'm doing."

"How the hell did you know I was talking about you?"

"I could hear your brain working overtime," she retorted.

The security guard then beckoned to the three of them.

"Mr Lyon is ready to see you. Please take the lift to the fifth floor. Mr Lyon's office is the second door on the right: his secretary is expecting you."

The Reverend pressed the call button and they soon entered the lift. It was an old-fashioned conveyor with an outer gate concealing an inner metal shutter door you had to draw across in order to initiate the mechanism. Instead of an LCD counter a brass arm moved clockwise across a dial. Dai declared that he would count off its digits in French to ensure they exited at the right floor.

So, as the lift ascended Dai commenced an "un, deux, trois, pedwar, pump" without realising his linguistic lapse into Welsh.

When the lift stopped they exited.

"Did you know that you started in French and ended in Welsh, Dai?" enquired the Reverend.

"Well, even if I did I still got us to the right floor didn't I? Look, there's the door."

Dai knocked and walked straight in, to be met by Mr Lyon's secretary.

"Good morning. Please take a seat for one moment. I will let Mr Lyon know you're here."

She then knocked on an inner door and awaited an acknowledgement before walking into Mr Lyon's office and shutting the door behind her. Shortly, the door re-opened.

"Please come in," invited the secretary. "Mr Lyon is ready for you."

Mrs Morgan Morgan entered first followed by the Reverend and then Dai. Mr Lyon was standing in front of his desk and extended his hand in greeting.

"Good morning. Pleased to meet you."

Mrs Morgan Morgan duly introduced herself as did the Reverend. It was then Dai's turn.

"Hello Mr Lion! How are you?"

Mr Lyon looked at him with sensitivity.

"Excuse me, sorry: it's not 'Lion', it's 'Lyon'," he articulated, spelling out each letter.

"'L-y-o-n'" repeated Dai in apology. "Well, mine is 'David', D-a-v-i-d: pronounced 'Dai'."

"Er...yes. Please make yourself comfortable."
He gestured to the leather three-piece suite while he made for a leather armchair.

"I have taken the liberty of ordering us some tea as I know you English like your tea. Is that OK?"

"I prefer coffee as I'm Welsh not English, mun. It's like me saying you're German and not Belgium."

"Oh, I'm so sorry! I hope I did not upset you. Please excuse me."

"I will forgive you just this once," intoned Dai with solemnity.

"So, I hear that you Welsh are rugby-mad? I went to Cardiff once and saw your Cardiff Arms Park."

Once again Dai felt bound to correct him.

"It's the Millennium Stadium now, butte."

"Once again, I can only apologise. I did not know it had changed."

"The old Arms Park got knocked down years ago. They built the new stadium in 1999, I think it was, but they thought that the because of the way British workmen could be that they would not have finished it 'til the new millennium. That's why they called it 'The Millennium Stadium' and not the '1999 Stadium'."

There was then a knock at the door. In entered Mr Lyon's secretary carrying a full tray of refreshments.

"Thank you, Nicole," replied Mr Lyon, to which Dai could not resist adding "Papa", recalling the old Renault advert. Mr Lyon appeared momentarily confused but politely returned to his hot cup of tea.

"So, please tell me how I can help you? I will try to do my utmost to solve your problem."

"Do you have any more appointments today?" asked Mrs Morgan Morgan. "If you do, may I suggest that you cancel them as this is a long story that needs a quick solution. I will start from the very beginning."

Dai observed Mr Lyon's surprise.

"You should have asked for a flask of tea as one cup's not going to be enough for you, boyo!"

Two hours of explanation were only broken by the Reverend filling Mrs Morgan Morgan's rare pauses for breath with Hell-fire invectives against the perpetrators of his village's proposed identity change.

Dai meanwhile pondered whether the year 1987 had anything to do with why Brynlog hated Aberglas so much? The local rugby final between the two teams ended with Aberglas running out 50 points to 3 winners. It was a crushing humiliation for Brynlog and Dai thought that they still bore the grudge.

"Some people are so childish. Life's too short," he declared, without revealing to the other three that he had not spoken to former junior school friend, Wilf Francis, for over 45 years. Wilf had apparently beaten him in a game of marbles, winning all of Dai's off him. Dai still hoped that Wilf would one day drive through the village and stop at the *Dragon and Daff* so that Dai could ban him for life. He had no idea where Wilf resided but he still lived in hope.

Mr Lyon had taken notes throughout the meeting and after more cups of tea he finally put his pen and paper down.

"OK, I see your problem but may I ask what you would like me to help you with?"

This time the Reverend actually managed to squeeze in a sentence.

"We were hoping you would be able to assist us as you did with the other village many years ago."

Mr Lyon looked confused.

"I'm sorry. I still don't understand."

"Listen, butte," interjected Dai. "Remember when you helped the village of Kilbride? No, hang on a minute. It's not Kilbride...what is it again?"

"He means Killesberg," tutted Mrs Morgan Morgan.

"I was close though. They both begin with the letter 'K'.

"So does 'Kathmandu'."

"You remember," continued Dai, ignoring her correction, "when you stopped them being twinned with another town?"

Finally Mr Lyon understood.

"Now I comprehend you but I am so sorry: you have got the wrong Phillipe Lyon. You actually want my older brother Phillipe Christien Lyon. I am actually Phillipe Claude Lyon."

"You mean we have wasted the last two days of our lives on the wrong brother?" snapped Mrs Morgan Morgan.

"Did your Father want policemen in the family?" laughed Dai.

"I'm sorry? I don't understand."

"Well, both sons' initials are 'P.C.' Lyon."

Mr Lyon remained baffled.

"If my Father had wanted us to be law enforcement officers we would have been called 'Gendarmes'. That is what law enforcement officers over here are called."

"But if you were born in Wales you would have been 'PCs'."

"What is the point of this argument?" interrupted Mrs Morgan Morgan.

"No reason. I was just saying, that's all."
Mr Lyon once again spoke up.
"I apologise for the misunderstanding but I can give you the address of my brother's office. It is in Strasbourg, France, if you would like it?"
"You told me and the Reverend that you were right!" sneered Dai to Mrs Morgan Morgan.
"Well, it does not matter anyway, does it? We can't go to France as we don't have the air fare."
Mr Lyon rose from his chair.
"Let me just check something please."
He commenced a communication and then printed it out for them.
"OK, just let me read through this and see if I can help you the same way as my brother did."
He perused some related correspondence for a few moments, still deep in thought.
"Indeed, my brother did help the village of Killesberg but I have now read the full report and it states that four years later, after a second court hearing, their government actually won the appeal forcing Killesberg to rejoin their original country. They were then obliged to twin with another town. Their government stated that due to the village actually being under their rule that they did not have the power to defy them. Therefore, they fought for four years but eventually lost."
"Yes, OK but they were foreign - not Welsh. We will fight 'til the bitter end, won't we?"
Both Mrs Morgan Morgan and the Reverend nodded in agreement.
"I understand your feelings and apprehension," continued Mr Lyon, undeflected, "in having to twin with an unfamiliar town but if this article is correct I am sorry but you don't stand much of a chance winning."
"So, Mr Lyon," mused the Reverend, "there is nothing we can do whatsoever? You are saying that we just have to accept that we are doomed? Well, so much for freedom and democracy! As always, the smallest always loses."
"The only way I could see you being able to beat your government would be if you were like Monaco."

"Well, that's a bit of a stupid statement!" retorted Mrs Morgan Morgan.

Suddenly Dai had an idea.

"Hang on a minute. What do you mean Mr Lyon: 'if we lived in Monaco'?"

Mr Lyon patiently explained to the assembled crowd that Monaco was actually its own Principality despite many people thinking it belonged to France.

"You little beauty! No, better than that: you're a legend, butte!"

They all looked at Dai.

"You all right?" asked the Reverend of him. "Jetlag returned, has it?"

"No. Am I the only one here who understands what we must do?"

The others nodded.

"This man is a genius," he proclaimed pointing at Mr Lyon.

Mr Lyon smiled and thanked Dai but still requested an explanation.

"Honest. It's so easy, even a child could understand it. But there's never one around when you want one! Same as about a month ago: Megan bought a new television cabinet that was flat-packed. It took me nearly four hours to put it together and it said on the instructions a child could build it in an hour. But they did not letter the pieces and I put the top on the bottom and the bottom on the top and everything…"

Mrs Morgan Morgan just had to interrupt him.

"I for one don't care about your battle with your stupid coffee table! What are you talking about?"

"First of all," glowered Dai, "it was a television cabinet and not a coffee table. Coffee tables are easy: four legs on the floor with the table on top of it. Even a child could do it."

"Would it be possible for you to actually let us in on your brainwave before it gets dark or we die of old age?" pleaded Mrs Morgan Morgan with exasperation.

"I think I know what your brainwave is," declared the Reverend.

"At last," breathed out Dai, "another intelligent human being. Thank God for that."

"But I won't take your glory, Dai. You can explain to the other two."

In actual fact the Reverend did not have a clue. However, if Dai assumed that he did then maybe he would actually explain the idea to all of them - before it went dark or they did indeed all die of old age.

Dai stood up as if he was preaching to the flock like the Reverend did on a Sunday.

"Well, as Mr Lyon said," at this point gesturing elaborately towards him, "he said the only way to be able to beat the government was to live in Monaco."

"We are not moving the village to Monaco, you silly man!" shouted Mrs Morgan Morgan.

"Hush mun," snapped Dai. By now he was so hyped he did not realise his tone towards her – until he caught her evil glare.

"Sorry! I did not mean it the way it came out. I apologise. What I meant to say was, could I please ask you to refrain from talking 'til I have finished my statement? Thank you, Diane."

At this point the Reverend had to prevent Mrs Morgan Morgan from getting up and hitting him with her large handbag.

"Calm down! You will love me for this if you give me a chance to speak," beamed Dai.

The Reverend looked towards the window. Dai noticed.

"What's up, Rev?"

"Sorry. I was just checking it was still light."

Dai smiled weakly at this but it did slightly relieve the tension.

"I agree it would be a stupid idea to move to Monaco. After all, none of us can speak Monaco-ese. But we could take a leaf out of their books and become our own independent country. It's simple. Then we could tell Brynlog to go blow it out their ass."

The Reverend looked at Dai with disgust.

"Sorry! I meant to say, 'Stick it up their jumper!'"

It was the first time that Dai had sworn all trip. He was so proud of himself until then. Even when the plane was bouncing up and down he had managed to keep his language clean. However, had he been able to have regained the power of speech first thing this morning he would have had to have put about £50 in the swear-jar after the way the Reverend had awoken him.

"That has got to be the most stupid idea I have ever heard," declared Mrs Morgan Morgan looking to the Reverend for agreement. "I knew we should not have let you come with us, David the Public House."

"Hold on one moment. It actually sounds like a plan. Please continue Dai."

"Cheers Rev," Dai exclaimed in excitement.

Mr Lyon walked back to his computer.

"Well, there must be a way of becoming an independent country? Then we can make our own rules and regulations and nobody from outside, like Brynlog, can do anything about it. We will be our own little Wales in Wales - bit like Saint David's down on the East coast."

"Sorry Dai," interrupted the Reverend, "but Saint David's is actually on the West coast of Wales."

"Nobody told me they had moved it!" laughed Dai. "Anyway, this is the greatest idea since somebody decided to put beans on toast [Dai's favourite food] so there you go: problem solved. When we go home it won't be just to Wales but also to little Wales, our new country. I thank you."

Dai duly took a bow, sat back down and tapped himself on the back. He had not been this excited since Megan and her sister had gone to their cousin's funeral in Cornwall and had decided to stay, giving Dai a whole night of freedom. He had come up with so many ideas as to what he was going to do that he had asked Glenys Jenkins, who sometimes helped them behind the bar, to work the Saturday night. Dai was going to go to Brynlog and meet up with Dai the Inn, in his words "to have a good session and then afterwards have a curry".

The *Dragon and Daff* did not have any type of curry on the menu as Megan said that it was not proper food, so refused to prepare it. Dai had even asked Megan to make it instead in their own private kitchen but Megan staunchly held out stating that it would stink the place out. What made things worse for Dai was the fact that there was no Indian or Chinese takeaway in Aberglas. Therefore he could only get a real curry in Brynlog. Dai decided that as it was going to be a heavy drinking night, finished off with a curry, that he would have a long bath followed by a couple of hours sleep so that he would be refreshed and ready to party. Unfortunately, Dai had forgotten to set his alarm. He awoke at 11.20pm.

The *Drag and Daff* had been so quiet that evening that Glenys had locked up just after 10pm. Therefore instead of having a good session and a curry he found himself sat in the bar with a pint of bitter and a packet of pork scratchings: 'Nothing like living the high life', he thought to himself.

Mr Lyon pressed the print button on his computer and rejoined the others.

"OK. I have just checked up on how to become an independent country. The best example I could find was by going back to before the American Civil War. Here the Confederation declared independence from the rest of America and forced people to recognise them."

"Now, hang on a minute," interrupted the Reverend. "Didn't that start the American Civil War? We don't want any bloodshed thank you very much."

"OK. What about the independent countries that were formed when the Iron Curtain fell?"

"Well, actually they were never really part of the USSR," replied Mr Lyon.

"Hang on now," resumed Dai. "You don't really think that Brynlog will declare war on us, do you? Because if they did, we would be OK. Anyway, as for a start we haven't got a beach: so they can't come by boat. Also we don't have a airport, so they would have to land at Cardiff International and drive over to us from there. It would take them over two hours to get to us from Cardiff when it normally only takes about 20 minutes from Brynlog by car."

Dai was now in full swing.

"If they decided to invade us by road instead we could put up a toll bridge and charge them £10 to come over. They would have to pay the maximum like they charge on the Severn crossings. And at least if they did invade us by road, the money we got from them we could buy our own tanks and we would not have to pay on the way out!"

"But we would have to pay on the way back, though!" laughed the Reverend.

"Don't be a div. If they tried to charge us we could blow the toll booth up!"

Dai burst out laughing at the thought.

"This is getting so stupid!" announced Mrs Morgan Morgan. "I have had enough! I'm leaving."

As she stood up she smiled at Mr Lyon.

"Well, I came here with hope but instead you have left me hopeless. Thank you very much."

With that she turned around and left the room. The Reverend put his hand out thank Mr Lyon for his time and attention, apologising for Mrs Morgan Morgan but affirming her deep-down gratitude for his help and honesty. The Reverend then picked up his coat, folded it over his arms and followed her outside.

Dai shook his head at the closed door.

"Well, I still think our idea is great and I'm sure it's going to work. Those two will come around eventually. Can I have those papers you printed off please, for future reference?"

"I'm sorry the other two don't seem to understand what you are trying to do."

"Well, I think the Reverend's OK but it's the Dragon that's the main problem."

Dai stretched his hand out to shake Mr Lyon's hand.

"I have to apologise as well on behalf of Mrs Morgan Morgan. She has a rare condition. It's actually terminal: it's called 'misery guts'", and as Dai shook Mr Lyon's hand they both laughed loudly.

Nicole smiled him a farewell and pleasant stay in her country.

"Cheers sweetheart. You have a good one too...and don't forget at the end of the day: it's night!"
He winked at her and then left.

"You English are very silly with your sayings!" she replied.

"Yes, the English are very silly," replied Dai, "but us Welsh aren't! Remember love, we were born with music in our blood and a song in our hearts. This is not goodbye: it's 'Tarah love'."

At the lift Mrs Morgan Morgan simply stared at Dai.

"That has got to be the most stupidest idea I have ever heard - and the Reverend agrees with me, don't you?"
Before the Reverend could open his mouth, Mrs Morgan Morgan concluded, "See, he does."

At the ground floor the Reverend asked the security guard to request a taxi for them. Shortly afterwards they were on their way back to the hotel. The Reverend suggested a nice cup of tea and perhaps some relaxation before going to see the Cathedral. They therefore made their way to the bar where Dai ordered a pot of tea for Mrs Morgan Morgan, a coffee for the Reverend - and a pint of Stella Artois for himself. He brought the drinks to the table, prompting a huff from Mrs Morgan Morgan.

"Typical! You can't sit in a bar without having something alcoholic."

"This time it was not my fault. As I went up to the bar, serving behind it was the same barman as last night. He poured the Stella before I could ask for a coffee."

"Dai, you could have refused the Stella and told him he had made a mistake."

"I would have but what you don't realise, Mrs Morgan Morgan, is that you have never worked in the pub trade. Therefore you would not know that if, by any chance, you make a mistake and pour the wrong drink, you have to pay for it yourself and then drink it. Now, it's OK for me as I'm my own boss when Megan's not there but if that poor chap had to drink it, his boss might have seen him and sacked him for drinking on the job. So basically I just saved his job for him."

The Reverend sat there impressed: anytime that Dai got into trouble he would always talk himself out of the situation. It always amazed the Reverend: in all the years he had known Dai, he had never seen him flustered or lost for words.

"I often think you should have been a politician."

"You won't believe me but I was going to but I spelt it wrong on the job application form. I wrote 'Publican' instead."

The two of them laughed. Mrs Morgan Morgan looked on in disgust so Dai decided to change the subject.

"What time's the flight home?"

"We depart at 9.40 this evening," she replied, retrieving the information from the bowels of her handbag.

"Plenty of time to revisit the Cathedral, then?" suggested the Reverend.

"I don't think I'm in the mood to sightsee. I can feel one of my heads coming on. Anyway, David the Public House is back in his favourite place here so I assume he would not like to go again anyway?"

"Excuse me," he replied with mock disgust, "but I'm quite willing to revisit the Cathedral. It was lovely to behold. So, Reverend, it would be a pleasure."

"Thank you David. It would be a privilege to accompany you also."

Mrs Morgan Morgan looked at the pair of them.

"You're just saying that to try to make me feel better. Now please excuse me as I need to visit the ladies' bathroom."

The Reverend smiled at Dai.

"Everyday you amaze me with the way you think on your feet - like the lager situation there and also the fact that you are willing to visit the Cathedral again."

"Well, being married to Megan you have always got to be two moves ahead. It is like living with a chess champion sometimes - and also I really liked the Cathedral yesterday." Dai took a sup of his lager and pulled a funny face.

"That's better. It did not kill me last night and hopefully it will cure me today. But I must ask you something: if we do revisit the Cathedral again today, could we go up the same street as yesterday as I did see a lovely bar with sofas in, and is there any chance of us visiting that as well?"

"Well Dai, as you said yesterday, it would be a pity to come all they way to Brussels just to sit in the hotel bar. We might as well try a different one before we go home."

At this point Mrs Morgan Morgan returned to her chair.

"Is everything OK?" enquired the Reverend.

"Why shouldn't it be?" she snapped.

"Well," said Dai, "we just organised our revisit to the Cathedral so after you have finished your tea we will make our way there."

Closing her eyes Mrs Morgan Morgan stated that they would have to go without her: "I have a terrible headache."

"Hangover started, has it?"

"If you suffered the same as I do with headaches, you would not be so quick off the mark to make a joke. I am going to retire to my room. I will meet you in here at five this evening to have an early supper before we leave for the airport."

Without another word she rose and headed for her room.

"Well, I assume she will not be coming with us then?"

"Two's company, three's a crowd - and a right miserable one at that. Do you know, I think she is just faking having a headache just so she does not have to come with us. She's cutting her nose off to spite her face."

"Well, actually I was thinking that myself. You know what they say Dai? Great minds think alike."

"Well how did us two think alike then?" smirked Dai.

Two hours later they returned from the Cathedral heading towards the pub with the sofas Dai had seen yesterday. They went up to the bar. Dai requested a pint of Stella and large glass of wine.

"No thanks Dai. I will have a cup of coffee not a wine."

"You do know that later on this evening we are going to have to sit next to the Dragon for three hours on a plane and without any means of escape? If it's anything like it was yesterday…"

"Well thought of Dai. Do you sell bottles of wine?" reconsidered the Reverend turning to the barman, also reflecting that it might actually be cheaper overall to buy the bigger unit.

"Do you think it's a stupid idea trying to become independent from the rest of Wales? Be honest now, it's only me and you."

"The thing is, Dai, we are too small to be taken seriously. We would end up being the laughing stock of Wales and also the United Kingdom. It would never work but it was a great idea though."

Dai looked crestfallen. Then all of a sudden a thought came to him.

"But what about David and Goliath? Nobody thought David would win and yet he knocked him out in round one. Now, if the Bible states he did it, then why can't we? You're a man of the cloth so you know the story better than me."

"There is one thing you never have to do to me, Dai, and that is preach the Bible. I know the story but can you honestly say that we have a fighting chance? I know everyone loves an underdog but think with your head not with your heart, boyo."

"Do you remember Wrexham in the FA Cup? They beat the mighty Arsenal, they did. Micky Thomas: what a goal, and you can never forget the greatest comeback in history: the England versus Wales match at Wembley. Losing half time, then our Scott Gibbs..." and Dai put his hands together as if he was going to pray again, "...I mean Saint Scott Gibbs, went over the try line."

Dai put his arm up in the air just like Scott Gibbs had done scoring that try.

"Well, you make a good argument Dai but can you put your hand on your heart and truthfully say we have a fighting chance?"

"Better than that, Rev. I swear on my drinking arm that I believe we have a fighting chance!"

The Reverend laughed.

Anyway," resumed Dai, "with you on my side everyone will vote for it."

"I know that I stand there every Sunday preaching the rights and wrongs but even though I'm the Reverend, it does not mean that they will vote with us."

"No, it's not that. That's not the reason why they would come on our side. It's not the fact that you're our Reverend. It's because if they vote against us you can condemn them all to Hell."

Holding this thought, Dai raised his glass.

"Well: nothing ventured nothing gained."

"In that case," the Reverend sighed, "count me in boyo, count me in."

"Tidy, mun. If we got God and you on our side, the world doesn't stand a chance."

Chapter Seven

Back Home

It was just gone 4.30pm when Dai and the Reverend returned to their room to pack. Dai removed his suit, shirt and tie and folded them neatly on the bed before stuffing them into his sports bag. He changed into his jeans and polo shirt.

"That's me done," he triumphantly declared as the Reverend was still only placing his second shirt in his suitcase. Dai looked at the way the Reverend was packing all his clothes neat and tidily.

"You might as well just chuck it in. By the time we get to the other end it's going to be creased anyway."

"Well that might be so but at least it won't be through any fault of my own."

Dai checked the bedside cabinet to make sure he had not forgotten anything. Then he looked at the Reverend.

"I got to ask you: these Gideons, do they visit every hotel room in the world?"

"You have just found one of their Bibles, haven't you?"

"Yep, it is here but you would think though that remembering to visit every hotel room in the world they would actually remember to take their Bibles home with them afterwards."

"Well then, I suggest you put it back in the drawer in case they remember and come back for it then."

Dai replaced it and then looked at his watch.

"It's quarter to five. I'm going to go down and grab a pint before the Dragon gets there. See you later."

With that he flung his bag over his shoulder and headed downstairs towards the bar.

Dai sat at his usual table and was halfway through his pint when Mrs Morgan Morgan entered.

"Have you been here all afternoon, David the Public House?"

"And a good afternoon to you too! I will have you know that actually we went and visited the Cathedral again. It was very refreshing."

Dai decided he was going to use 'refreshing' now instead of saying 'We also went to the pub'.

The Reverend soon joined them and they ordered their bar meals. Dai was still on the lager, Mrs Morgan Morgan drank tea and - according to Dai and the Reverend - the Reverend was enjoying his first glass of wine of the day. In a way this was true because at the other bar he had ordered a bottle, not a glass.

The taxi picked them up outside the hotel and just after seven they passed through the departure doors at Brussels airport, ready for home. If Dai and the Reverend had their way, the next time anyone from Aberglas returned from holiday to Wales, it would be as a different country. But that prospect seemed a long way off at the moment. Yet as Dai had said, "With God on their side there would be no problems".

They headed for the Fly Us check-in desk. The airport was a lot busier than it had been at Cardiff the day before; also only one person at a time could approach that desk unless accompanying a child. There was a line on the floor which you could only cross after being called to the desk, to prevent an invasion of privacy.

Dai checked in first, with a feeling of dread as to what would happen when it was Mrs Morgan Morgan's turn. He hoped he had come up with an ingenious way of preventing a recurrence of the scene in Cardiff airport, so spoke in a voice that only the check-in attendant could hear.

"Listen love. The woman behind me made a lot of fuss yesterday at Cardiff airport, so please can you do us both a favour?"

The attendant looked intrigued.

"Will you just pretend that this note is for her?"

Dai passed the lady a note he had written at the hotel bar before Mrs Morgan Morgan and the Reverend had rejoined him. She smiled.

"I don't think I'm allowed to do that, sir."

"For your sake and mine it will be the easiest way. Trust me."

"OK. I will do it if it's the easiest way."

Dai winked and thanked her.

"Next please."

Up stepped Mrs Morgan Morgan and handed her passport over. The attendant opened it and then surveyed her.

"Good evening, Mrs Morgan Morgan. Excuse me, I have a message for you."

She picked up Dai's note and pretended that it really did come from the Captain:

> *To Mrs Morgan Morgan,,*
> *May I, on behalf of the cabin crew and from the flight desk, thank you for travelling with us. I found out what flight you were booked on for your return journey back to Cardiff so I made sure that I would be flying you back home. Please have a pleasant journey.*
> *Kind regards,*
> *Captain Jones*

"Thank you very much, and I will thank Mr Jones when I see him."

Dai blew the woman a kiss in thanks.

After the Reverend checked in it was time to deal with the dreaded security scan. Dai had remembered this time to remove his belt and stood there with his hands in his pockets, trying to hold his jeans up.

"You had better go first, David the Public House, as you will most probably set off that alarm again. The Reverend and myself will then meet you in the refreshment area when you have finished being interrogated."

She moved aside so that Dai could go first.

"Next please," shouted the guard.

Dai held his breath, stood up straight and walked towards the scanner. He was still holding his breath – and his trousers - then closed his eyes: no alarms. He turned around to Mrs Morgan Morgan and poked his tongue out at her like a little boy. Mrs Morgan Morgan pretended she did not see him.

"Next please," requested the guard again. This time Mrs Morgan Morgan walked through – setting off the alarm.

"Excuse me, madam. Please come this way," ordered a female guard.

Dai would never forget the look on Mrs Morgan Morgan's face as she was being hand-scanned: it was a mixture of horror and anger. The Reverend meanwhile passed through it without a problem.

"Told you they would catch you! Give them the cocaine. You might get time off your prison sentence if you do!" yelled Dai back to Mrs Morgan Morgan.

"Move away, Dai. You are not helping the situation." Dai, however, could not go anywhere as he was laughing so much. Wiping away his tears with both hands he did not realise that his jeans had slipped down to the end of his boxer shorts.

"Niice boxers, butte," sniggered the Reverend.

Dai grabbed at his jeans to pull them up but did it so quickly that he nearly squashed what he called 'Megan's wedding present', and would have ended up walking as if he had been horseriding for a day without a saddle.

Meanwhile Mrs Morgan Morgan found herself having a heated discussion with the female guard. It was so loud that everyone could hear her.

"How dare you do this to me! Don't you know I'm British? I want your name and serial number. Don't you realise this airport will be in chaos if you don't let me through! Captain Jones will not fly his plane back to Cardiff if I am not on it. It's on your head, young lady."

The female guard seemed unfazed. She was used to it even if Mrs Morgan Morgan had now made it to her top-five list of all-time rudest passengers. She scanned the back of Mrs Morgan Morgan. The culprit was just below Mrs Morgan Morgan's sleeve: for some reason there was a tiny paper clip attached to her. The guard held it forth for Mrs Morgan Morgan to see.

"Well it's not mine! Do you think I would try and smuggle through a paper clip, you stupid girl?"

"Thank you, madam. Enjoy your flight," was the rejoinder followed by a silent 'I hope your plane ride is like a roller coaster all the way home'.

Mrs Morgan Morgan walked over to the others. Dai had refused to budge because he had been enjoying the show too much. The Reverend calmly took Mrs Morgan Morgan's arm.

"Let's get you a cup of tea to calm your nerves."

"And put a bloody double brandy in it as well," requested Mrs Morgan Morgan.

The Reverend looked shocked.

"Oh grow up man! 'Bloody' is in the Bible. If you don't believe me, check it yourself."

With that Mrs Morgan Morgan stormed off towards the Ladies' room just past the security checkpoint. Dai and the Reverend headed towards the bar.

"I can't believe she swore. I have never ever since I have known her, heard her swear in front of me!"

"That's not swearing, Rev. *This* is swearing…"

He opened his mouth but before he could say anything the Reverend put his finger to Dai's lips.

"Be like the lions in Daniel's den and keep your mouth closed David, please."

"That's one of my favourite songs from Sunday School."

Instead of swearing, he started singing his favourite childhood song. After the first line the Reverend joined in.

Dai then went to the bar while the Reverend found them a table. Dai had ordered a lager for himself, a large wine for the Reverend and a French coffee [brandy-infused] for Mrs Morgan Morgan. Informed of the price he unfurled a Euro note from his wallet for the bartender before reconsidering his intended action.

"Can I give you my Euro coins in my pocket instead so I can get rid of them?"

Dai then grabbed a mixture of Euros and Cents out of his pocket. He picked out the total and put the remaining couple of coins back in his pocket before making his way with the drinks back to the table where the Reverend was sitting. Mrs Morgan Morgan had still had not returned.

"I hope she is OK. She seemed really flustered and nearly lost her temper completely. That's the worst I have ever seen her in all the time I have known her."

"Talking about losing things," mused Dai, "I just emptied my pocket to get rid of all the Euro coins I have had since I got here and I can't find my lucky paper clip."

"David," replied the Reverend gravely. "Are you trying to tell me that you lost your lucky paper clip? May I ask where you had it last?"

"Well, I was standing behind Mrs Morgan Morgan before the metal detector and then she told me to go in front of her. That's the last time I saw it."

He could no longer sustain his innocence.

"That's it, Dai. You will now definitely go to Hell for that one. There's nothing I can do to save your soul."

"Well, I may endure eternal torture but it will be worth it. Funniest thing I seen since those Americans ate at my pub!"

Mrs Morgan Morgan took ten minutes to rejoin them.

"Are you all right Mrs Morgan Morgan? You have been a very long time."

"I did not know you were timing me," she growled to the Reverend.

"I was only concerned about you, that's all."

"Well, if you must know, I was looking for the owner of this airport so that I can make an official complaint about that stupid little jumped-up girl."

Dai passed Mrs Morgan Morgan her coffee.

"Calm down, mun. She was only doing her job. Don't make such a fuss about it. I didn't look for the owner of Cardiff's airport when it happened to me and I did not kick up a fuss either."

Mrs Morgan Morgan merely glared at Dai.

"It is different when it happens to the likes of you as no doubt when people like you fly, it's expected. And another thing: I am not talking to you, David the Public House, after that comment you made about the Coca Cola."

"Two things, Diane..." If she was not talking to him she could not shout at him for calling her 'Diane' he reasoned. "First of all, it was not Coca Cola. It was 'cocaine' and second of all, how can you tell me you're not talking to me as you *are* talking to me to tell me you're not talking to me?"

"Don't be so childish. I am making a statement to confirm to you that I'm not talking to you. And if you carry on, I will tell Captain Jones not to allow you to fly - and then you will have to find an alternative way to get home! So if you want to fly home on the flight, I suggest you sit there and shut up until we arrive back in Wales."

"Changing the subject," interrupted the Reverend, "may I just say that despite not getting the answer we had hoped from Mr Lyon, that it has still been a very pleasant two days. Please do not sour it by having this meaningless argument. Let's just get back to Aberglas. Then, if you two choose not to speak to each other ever again, that's fine but can you please just be civil for the flight home?"

"No problem, Rev. I agree with you."
The two of them then looked at Mrs Morgan Morgan. She glanced at Dai, and then back at the Reverend, smiled and then snarled, "No chance".

After what seemed an eternity of silence, their flight was called. They made their way to Gate 12 and eventually boarded the craft. They were not seated together this time: Mrs Morgan Morgan found herself by the window in Row 18, next to the Reverend, while Dai had been allocated a seat in Row 14. Apparently a family of four had been on stand-by for the flight. Luckily for them the passengers originally scheduled for the flight had failed to appear at the airport in time. The four did have to be split up from each other, though, with the Father being given the seat that Dai now occupied. However, Dai had no hesitation in offering up his place so that the family could all sit together. As for the three of them, the Reverend remained unsure as to who actually was the happiest but at least he now would not have to endure Dai's and Mrs Morgan Morgan's continued bickering.

The engines started up and the aircraft reversed from its gate. Once again the cabin crew demonstrated the standard emergency procedures before the Captain announced that all window shades had to remain open and the lights dimmed.

Dai pressed the call button above his head and one of the cabin crew approached.

"May I help you, sir?"

"Why are you dimming the lights? What's wrong? Is the plane OK?"

"The plane is fine. It's just that if for some reason we crash on take-off, your eyes will already be adjusted to the dark. So it will help with the evacuation. There's nothing to worry about, sir."

She smiled and returned to her jump seat. Dai wished he had just accepted the fact that the lights would be dimmed, with no questions asked. The engines then roared to maximum power, the brakes were released and the plane sped down the runway, gradually ascending. The power seemed to drop a little but then reverted. Dai closed his eyes and once again gripped the armrests.

"Stupid time to change gear," he thought to himself. "Why didn't he wait 'til we got level - or better still bought an airplane with automatic gears on it? Just 'Park', 'Reverse' and 'Forward'. It would be much safer. Next time I get to go on a plane, I'm going to make sure it has automatic gears."

While he was thinking this the plane began to level. The cabin crew rose from their seats and moved around the craft. The seatbelt sign soon disappeared and Dai opened his eyes for the first time since take off. He was relieved to find everyone still alive - including himself.

The two passengers next to him were a couple in their mid-70s. The husband occupied the seat by the window; his wife sat next to Dai. She smiled at him.

"You OK? I guess you don't like flying but don't worry. I am the same. I wish I could find another way to get to places. After all, if the Lord had wanted us to fly he would have given us wings."

Dai nodded. "I'm not scared of flying at all. I just don't like the take-offs, the landings and the bits in between. But I find if I close my eyes that my ears don't pop. I'm Dai by the way."

"Mary."

"No, I'm not Mary: I'm Dai. You're Mary."

They both laughed.

Mary's husband, Len, was already fast asleep. As they chatted she explained that Len took travel tablets to stop him feeling sick. The only problem was that they made him sleepy.

"It can therefore be quite boring for me without any company."

"Well if you do not like flying, why don't you also take some of the tablets to sleep through the flight?"

"I can't do that. If we were both asleep, we might miss our stop."

Bewildered, Dai just nodded anyway.

They were happily chatting away when once again the seatbelt sign became illuminated. The Captain announced impending bad weather that might cause some turbulence. Len, Mary and Dai had never actually unbuckled their seatbelts. Indeed, the only time they were removed was either for the toilet or disembarkation.

As the plane started to shudder its way through the bad weather Mary began crossing herself. With every bump Dai found himself doing the same. The turbulence soon faded and the plane started flying smoothly again, much to everyone's relief.

Dai pressed the button above his head once more and the same stewardess walked up to him.

"Yes sir?"

"Do you fly through bad weather on purpose just to make the flight more interesting or as a punishment for us flying with a cheap airline? Surely you know where the bad weather will be with all those gadgets in the pilots' room? Even the weather girl on television tells us and she doesn't use a computer, just a map on the screen behind her."

"I can assure you, sir, we do not do it on purpose or punishment. If it wasn't for yourself and others I would not have a job. Unfortunately, the reason we have to fly through bad weather sometimes is for fuel consumption and also we can not deviate from our flight path too much due to other air traffic around us."

"So, you're telling me that you don't have enough petrol to go the long way round? I'm sure if the pilot phoned to the other pilots in the air they would slow down and let him pull in front of them to avoid the bad weather."

The stewardess' smile became strained.

"Unlike being in a car, sir, we can not radio the other airlines and ask them to slow down so we can pull in front of them. Every flight has its own flight path to follow. It's not like motorway driving. And I have to tell you that very rarely do we suffer from any type of turbulence during flights."

"This is the second time in two days that I have flown with you and gone through turbulence, so you can't say it's very rare."

"Maybe you're just unlucky when it comes to flying? Now, if there is nothing else I can help you with, sir, I do have other passengers to attend."

Dai was suddenly struck by the thought that he had just sounded like Mrs Morgan Morgan. A shiver passed through him more violently than any turbulence.

The rest of the flight was uneventful. They landed at Cardiff just five minutes later than scheduled. Mrs Morgan Morgan exited at the front of the plane but not before stopping to request of the stewardess the presence of Captain Jones from the flight deck. She wished to thank him for the letter and also the flight. The stewardess appeared confused.

"I'm sorry. There must be a mix up. Captain Harries was your pilot this evening. Captain Jones was not on the flight."

Mrs Morgan Morgan was infuriated and stormed off down the steps, followed by the Reverend.

"I don't understand. He wrote me a letter. I assume he must have missed the flight. I knew it wasn't him flying us as it wasn't as good as the flight over."

Inside the terminal they met up with Dai again, now standing by the luggage carousel.

"Did you know it wasn't Captain Jones flying us this evening? Instead, it was a Captain Harries."

"Was it? I thought he wrote you a letter, Mrs Morgan Morgan? It might have been someone playing a joke on you just so you would not make a fuss and just get on the plane."

Mrs Morgan Morgan swung her handbag before either the Reverend or Dai could react, hitting Dai right in his arm.

"You're a horrible man, David the Public House!"
Dai rubbed his arm.

"Well, it worked didn't it? A little white lie is OK now and again!" he declared, looking at the Reverend for support.

"I'm staying out of this," replied the Reverend moving around the carousel, away from them both.

They picked up their suitcases and headed to the exit. Passing through the Nothing to Declare channel, Mrs Morgan Morgan turned around to Dai.

"You had better go through the other one and declare that you're an annoying, lying individual and should not be allowed back in Wales."

"Talking to me again now are we? Knew you could not resist my charm."

Mrs Morgan Morgan said nothing and made for the exit to meet Colin the Cabbie.

"Good trip was it? Did you sort it out? Are we OK or do we have to twin with another town?"

He did not pause for an answer as he opened the boot of his taxi.

"So, is it all sorted?" repeated Colin.

"All sorted, butte. But do you mind if we talk about it tomorrow? Bit tired tonight. Need to get our heads down."

"No problem. I completely understand. I know what you mean. I have only flown once - well twice, if you count coming back. Me and the wife went to Malta one year. Both had jetlag. Couldn't sleep for a couple of days afterwards. You get your head down. I will wake you when we get home."

The taxi pulled up outside the *Dragon and Daff* after dropping off Mrs Morgan Morgan and the Reverend. Dai grabbed his bag from the boot and tapped a farewell to Colin on the top of his cab.

Dai turned the key in the lock and walked into the bar, putting the lights on. He poured himself a lager, a large vodka and coke and went to sit down.

"Is that you Dai?" Megan shouted from upstairs.

"No, it's a thirsty burglar."

Megan made her way into the bar and looked at Dai with a pint in his hand.

"Thought you would have had enough of that over the last two days?"

Dai took a large swig and raised his glass.

"Missed you as well, my love."

Megan kissed Dai on the forehead.

"Welcome home, my love. Do you know what time it is? It's nearly 4am and I have to get up in three hours for the beer delivery. If I don't go back to bed now I will be waking up before I go to sleep. Glad you're home safely. If you decide to stay up for the delivery though, don't wake me. We can have a nice chat in the morning."

"It's morning now. It will be light soon."

Megan, however, had already started to make her way back upstairs to bed. Dai suddenly realised what Megan had said to him: if she didn't go back to bed now she would be awake before she fell asleep. He thought about it and again realised he had no idea what she meant.

The alarm went off and Megan hit the snooze button. She turned around and felt the outline of Dai lying next to her. She knew she would have to be the one to prepare for the beer delivery this morning so she got out of bed and went downstairs to put the kettle on. The kettle clicked off and Megan poured herself a cup of tea. She sat at the table drinking it until Dai appeared at the kitchen door.

"Well, if you knew you were going to get up for the delivery why did you make me get up as well?"

Dai pressed the kettle button again to make himself a coffee.

"I was going to have a lie-in but your alarm went off twice and I don't know how to shut it off. So I guess we are both awake now."

"If I had known you were going to wake up early though, I would not have set my alarm in the first place and *I* could have had a lie-in."

"If you had not set your alarm it would not have woken me up and *I* would have had a lie-in."

"But if I hadn't set it I would not have woken up and we would have missed the delivery. So to put it another way, we are both up so problem solved. Now, tell me all about your trip to the far-flung land of Belgium."

Dai missed out certain pieces of his recitation - mainly the pubs he had frequented and the quantities consumed - instead focusing on the meeting with Mr Lyon.

"Well, that was a waste of time then, and the chapel roof fund as well. Did you not think of researching a bit deeper before you left?"

"You were at the meeting. Everyone agreed that it was a good idea to go, including yourself. Do you think we would have gone over there for no reason? That would have been a complete waste of time and money."

"Maybe you just went there to be able to get away from me for the night?"

"Don't be such a div. If I had wanted to get away from you for a night I would not go all the way to Belgium. I would pay for you to go to Cornwall with your sister to see your cousin."

"Dai, you are so stupid: she died. We buried her, remember?"

"Doesn't mean you could not go down and visit her grave?"

Dai looked at his watch.

"The beer delivery will be here soon so I'm going to sort the cellar out."

He rose from his chair and headed for the cellar.

The Reverend sat in his kitchen reading the morning paper. The doorbell rang and there before him stood Dai.

"Morning, Rev. Kettle on, is it?"

"They say there's no rest for the wicked. Well, there's no rest for the good either. So what can I help you with this morning?"

"Well, we need to sort out a battle plan for the independence of Aberglas, don't we? So let's get the wheels in motion and fight the evil axis of Brynlog."

"Did you by any chance get home this morning and watch a war film before going to bed, Dai? I agree we can try and see if it's possible to gain some sort of independence from Brynlog but I would not call them an 'evil axis'. That was used when the Nazis came to power and I don't personally think that Brynlog Council will try to take over the world."

"I bet they said that about Hitler. First Aberglas, then America. You don't know what they are hiding behind closed doors. You heard of the KGB? Well, they could be the BGB: 'Brynlog' and what ever the 'G' and the 'B' stand for."

"So you're telling me that Brynlog might be the Welsh version of the KGB and you don't even know what the 'GB' stands for?" huffed the Reverend pouring the boiling water into his mug.

"Do you know what the 'GB' stands for then?"

"No, but I'm not saying that they are anything like them though."

"Well it could stand for 'Gestapo Branch' BGB?"

"Brynlog Gestapo Branch?"

"See, I told you I was right!"

"It's a pity we are still not in Belgium as I would be able to have a drink now."

"I think you are getting a bit of a drink problem, Rev."

"Well, it's a bit strange though that for some reason I only want a drink when I'm in your company."

"That's not nice, Rev. You're supposed to be a nice and kind man. I'm beginning to see a different side of you that's not nice. What would the villagers say if they found out what you're really like?"

"Don't think they would be as angry as Mrs Morgan Morgan if she ever found out about the great loss of your lucky paper clip!"

"Touché. Well, anyway how are we going to go about this? We can't just go in feet first. We need to be able to sell our idea to the rest of Aberglas."

"Our idea? I believe this was *your* idea, not *ours*'. I'm not going to be taking the blame for it if it goes wrong."

"Well, what happens if it goes to plan then?"

"In that case it was our idea then."

"You may be old and grey but you got your wits about you, I must admit."

"I will have you know it's not grey, it's silver. And you're right: I do have my wits and cunning about me. Maybe I should change my name to the Reverend Silver Fox?"

They both laughed and then set about working out a plan.

The Reverend got up went to one of the kitchen drawers to retrieve a large pad of paper and a pencil.

"I usually write my sermons on this. I find it easier to use a pencil as sometimes I make a mistake and need to erase it to ensure no-one reads it by accident."

"You mean, if you have forgotten to write down that all of us will burn in Hell for our sins? I know that is one of your favourite lines on a Sunday."

"Well, Dai. After your evil exploit upon the poor Mrs Morgan Morgan, I told you that you were condemned to Hell so you have nothing to worry: you're a certainty."

"The 'poor Mrs Morgan Morgan'? What do you mean 'poor'? You make her sound like an angel. The only angel she would be is the Angel of Death or a Hell's Angel. She will never be an angelic angel!"

"Well, if she is going to be a Hell's angel, that means she is going to keep you company in Hell for all eternity!"

Dai dropped to his knees in front of the Reverend. With hands clasped he prayed to the Reverend to be absolved of all his sins.

"Please have a word with your boss upstairs. Please tell him to let me into Heaven. I can't stand the thought of being with 'poor' Mrs Morgan Morgan for the rest of eternity. I will even give up drinking and betting and give all my money to orphaned donkeys or something else like that. Please help me!"

"First of all you told me that you don't bet. And are you are really going to give up drinking? Not a good start: lying to the man who's trying to save your soul."

"That's fair enough," muttered Dai, still on his knees. "How about I give some money to orphaned donkeys? One out of three isn't bad, is it?"

Dai put his hand on the chair to haul himself up from the floor. It promptly tipped on its side causing him to fall back down again.

"Tell you what, Rev. Why don't you join me down here? It's quite comfy."

After a second attempt Dai managed to clamber back into the chair.

"That's better. It was Hell down there!"

"No, Hell's a bit further down than that."

Dai stamped twice on the floor.

"Mrs Morgan Morgan? Are you there yet?"

"OK," laughed the Reverend. "Now to the serious stuff: how are we going to be able to convince the rest of the village that the best way forward is to gain independence from the rest of Wales?"

"Not just the rest of Wales, Rev, but the rest of the United Kingdom as well. There is no way we are just going to leave Wales. Could you imagine that if we left Wales and then got adopted by England instead we would have to follow the English rugby team and we can't do that! I like supporting a winning rugby side."

"But if we do leave the full United Kingdom you will not be able to support Wales as we will no longer be part of them anymore."

"Well, I support Brazil in the World Cup and I'm not Brazilian. I will just adopt Wales as my rugby team. It's OK though because my parents were born in Wales so I can do it through parentage. Wales have done it loads of times: one footballer who played for Wales actually qualified to play for them because his Nana once met Tom Jones in Merthyr Tydfil or something like that, so it's sorted. No problem. Right then, now that's sorted let's start the master plan!"

"First on the agenda: we need to have the answers to the questions that will be asked by the rest of the villagers. Now Dai: I will be myself and you can pretend to be one of the villagers, and after I have pretended to finish our plan you can ask any question or voice any concern you might think they will have. Do you understand?"

"No problem."

"So, ladies and gentleman, that is our proposal: to become independent. Now, does anyone have anything to say or ask? Yes? What is your question or concern?"

"I would just like to say that it's a fantastic idea, the best one I ever heard. Whoever thought it up should be made President of our new country and a statue erected in his honour so that people can lay flowers at his feet on his birthday and be worshiped for all eternity. See, told you it would be easy!"

"David! We need to be serious, otherwise we are finished before we even start! Now, stop messing about and take it seriously for once in your life. After all, it's your idea and if we fail it will not be your statue people will worship for years to come: instead they will talk about the idiot from the pub who tried and failed to make us independent! Now, which one would you prefer to be remembered by? Also, if there's a vote, *I* will end up being President, not *you*."

Dai seemed rather upset at the way the Reverend portrayed him so put his jokes aside for the time being. Over the next four hours the two of them sat there putting their proposal together. After several more cups of coffee and lots of brain-storming, they both seemed happy with the outcome.

"Now, we need to take this to Mrs Morgan Morgan for her opinion before we set a date for the meeting."

"That's not a good idea really, is it? The She-Devil thought it was a stupid idea and did not want anything to do with it. Don't you remember? She marched out of the office in disgust yesterday and also the three of us can't really sit down and discuss the issue as she is not talking to me."

"I'm sure she has forgiven you by now."

"You must be joking. She said yesterday that the next time she wants to speak to me is through a medium - which

I'm fine with as long as I am the one still alive and she is there in Hell where it's so hot that even Factor 3000 sun cream can't stop her getting burnt."

"If we don't have her as our ally we will have an almighty enemy instead. You know she is well respected in the village."

"Not respected, just feared more like. But if you can get her on our side it will be a miracle. I know the Lord works in mysterious ways but I think even he does not have much of a chance against her!"

"Let me just say, David," sighed the Reverend closing his eyes, "that the Lord does indeed as you say 'work in mysterious ways' but I think with his help we will get Mrs Morgan Morgan on our side. And just to tip the odds in our favour, I will ask her to join me for some refreshments after the service on Sunday. Then hopefully I will get her on our side because if we chat here, I have home advantage."

"The Silver Fox strikes again."

"Hmm. More importantly though, as soon as I finish the service on Sunday I would like you to leave as quickly as you can so you don't put her in a bad mood before my chat with her."

"Well, if you think it's better for me to go I will be out of here like a bat out of Hell or like an alcoholic heading to the bar at last orders."

The Reverend got up to answer a phone call.

"OK, I completely understand. No, no, honestly. If it's an emergency it will be done right away. Thank you for letting me know."

"What's wrong? Is everything all right, Rev? Is someone on their deathbed or has died already?"

"No, they have not died yet but it might be closer than they know. That was your Megan on the phone. She said that if you don't get back to the pub right away you will be dead. She is meeting Blodwyn in 20 minutes: it's her Bingo afternoon."

"Damn! Time flies when you're…"

"Having fun?" concluded the Reverend.

"No. When you're away from your wife! Right. I better go. Curfew is starting. Why don't you pop up for a wine later?"

"It's OK, Dai. The next time I have a wine now will most probably be at Christmas: the last two days were an exception. I did not want you to drink alone in a foreign country. That's the only reason why I partook in drinking with you."

"And also because Mrs Morgan Morgan was with us!" quipped Dai, shaking the Reverend's hand while running out of the door and all the way back to the pub. "Nothing like being the master of your own household", he thought as he made it to the pub in record time.

Chapter Eight

It will still rain

The meeting was arranged for the following Monday evening at the normal time of 7pm. Just after 6.15 Dai entered the hall. To his shock and surprise Mrs Morgan Morgan was already there, sitting next to the Reverend.

"Good evening Mrs Morgan Morgan."
"Hello David the Public House."
"How's it going, Rev?"
"Very good thank you, Dai. Are you OK though? You looked quite shocked when you came in."
"I think he is a bit surprised at my presence. You were expecting me to refuse to attend, I assume? Well, after the Reverend and myself had a discussion after the service on Sunday and also being offered the headship of our new independent government, I could simply not refuse."
"Head of the new government? We did not discuss that, Rev. And even if we did, I don't remember it and I thought at least we would have a vote and let the people decide. It's the fairest way as we don't want to become power crazy by just making up the rules ourselves. Don't want to be a dictatorship, do we?"

Mrs Morgan Morgan agreed with Dai - which came as an even bigger shock to him than when he walked in and saw her sitting there.

"You're right. We should have an election. No doubt I will win but if it makes you feel better, so be it. That is, of course, if the residents of our village vote to go independent in the first place. If they don't, then this whole exercise was a pointless waste of my time - and the chapel's roof fund!"
"Hang on. It was not just your time wasted but that of the three of us."
"Yes, there were the three of us but my time is more valuable than yours and the Reverend only works Sundays, so it did not affect him either."
"Excuse me, Mrs Morgan Morgan," interrupted the Reverend. "It's not just a Sunday job! I do a lot of work behind

closed doors also. I will have you know that I visit Brynlog hospital often to chat to the patients and I also visit Fallen Trees Nursing Home to meet with the residents there and give them spiritual guidance as they can no longer get out and go to chapel themselves."

"You mean you're helping them prepare for death, are you Rev? You're almost as bad as Mrs Morgan Morgan!"

Dai quickly realised that even he had gone too far this time.

"I did not mean anything by that. I don't mean that you murdered any of your husbands, honest!"

Dai could feel his blood starting to curdle as Mrs Morgan Morgan burnt into his soul the most evil look she had ever given anyone in public. The atmosphere could have been cut with a piece of soggy paper.

"Well then, hopefully we are all prepared for any questions that anyone asks. I'm hoping there won't be many. We will then request them to vote by the end of the month on the new head of our government and also if we are going to have a new village name or if we are going to stay as 'Aberglas'."

"You seem to be very certain that everyone is going to agree with our plan before they have even voted?" queried Morgan Morgan.

"He must be because he said if the plan does not work he was going to deny any responsibility and the whole blame would be put on my shoulders."

"Don't worry Dai! That is still the case. Anyway, as I was saying, we will also need to vote if we are going to be staying as a village or going to be a city or a town instead. We need to get everything in place before we tell the British government that we are no longer part of the United Kingdom."

At just past 7pm the village hall was packed. There were even people sitting on the floor between the aisles.

The Reverend stood up, cleared his throat and opened the meeting.

"Good evening my dearest friends."

This was nothing like the normal Sunday service address where they were never his 'friends' but rather 'Lambs of God' or 'Lambs to the slaughter'.

"I would like to thank you all for attending. We have compiled the results from our recent fact-finding mission to Brussels but unfortunately we did not get the results we were looking for. But we have come up with another idea which we hope you will agree on and to go forward with it, we will need at least 100% or more of you to agree to the proposal."

The Reverend duly outlined the plans, prompting a lot lot of murmuring amongst the crowd. No-one shouted or tried to halt proceedings while he spoke. At the end he thanked them for their attention and then invited anyone with any questions to raise them but as always to put their hand up first and only speak when they were acknowledged: "We don't want everyone shouting out at the same time."

The first hand raised was from Paula the Post.

"I must ask, if we go independent, will I still be able to use the Royal Mail? Also, will I need to issue different stamps as we can't really use the Queen's head on our stamps if we no longer belong to her country?"

"I will answer that one," interjected Dai. "Well, Paula, if we have to change the stamps' images they will have to be self-adhesive ones: if Mrs Morgan Morgan's face is on them there is no way I'm going to lick it!"

Mrs Morgan Morgan fumed and then stood up.

"If you have anything serious to ask then either the Reverend or myself will answer them. If you are just going to ask stupid questions, keep them to yourself until after the meeting has finished, and then you can have a chat with David the Public House. I hope I have made myself clear."

Once again Paula rose to her feet.

"My question is serious. It's my living. I need to know if my business will be OK, otherwise I'm will be voting 'No'."

"My dearest Paula," interrupted the Reverend, "we will not change the stamps, so you will be OK. It's just that we will have our own country but still use the United Kingdom's stamps, that's all."

Paula thanked the Reverend and sat back down. The Reverend remained on his feet awaiting the next question. This time it came from Sian the Shop.

"My question is, will we still be using the British currency we use now or are we going to have to get our own currency? It's a bit worrying as we know what has happened to some of the countries that now use the Euro. Also, I went to Spain once and I have also been to Egypt, and to be honest with you the money they use there is like Monopoly money. It does not seem real. Actually, we could use Monopoly money in our new country here as it's already in ones, fives, and tens et cetera."

"We didn't think of that, Dai," muttered the Reverend. Dai urged the Reverend to sit down and let him answer the question instead.

"That's a really good idea, Sian. Slight problem though: everyone here could go into Brynlog tomorrow and go to the toy shop and buy lots of Monopoly sets and become millionaires in half an hour. We will keep the same currency but will change the names from pence to 'Abers' so all coins up to a 50 will be 'Abers'. Then it will be '1 Glas', a '5-Glas', '10-Glas' and a '20-Glas'."

"What about a £50 note?" asked Sian.

"Well, if you got one of those you are one of the richest people here. I never seen one in my life but if you insist we will also have a '50-Glas'. Now, if anyone has a 50-Glas note on them could you please show me it afterwards? And don't worry, I will keep it safe in my wallet for you 'til the sun shines."

Next, Colin the Cabbie's hand went up.

"I know we got P.C. Williams as our first contact with the police but if he is on holiday we have always had the option of calling on Brynlog police. If we go independent they might not respond and also can I say I remember the Army once helping us out the year we had the heavy snow in the 90s. We could not get out to buy food and they gave us a ride on their trucks to Brynlog. I'm concerned they might decide not to help us either and we could starve to death or even worse than that."

"Well, we could stop P.C. Williams going on holidays," quipped Dai, "for the rest of his life or we could instead make up someone to deputise in his absence? Now, does anyone want to volunteer? If so, let us know by the end of the meeting and if you are successful, you will be known as 'Aberglas Special Constable' or A.S.C. for short. And with regards to the Army, unless the rest of the United Kingdom declares war on us, we don't really need a lot of soldiers but if anyone has a four-wheel drive and is able to get through snow to Brynlog for food and wishes to volunteer, you will be enlisted as Aberglas Special Soldiers, or A.S.S. for short."

The crowd burst into laughter. Dai was the only one there who did not get the joke. Indeed it was only when the Reverend quietly explained the initials to him that Dai realised he had said something funny.

"OK, maybe we will rethink the name of the Army. Anyone that does not think the Army should be an 'a-s-s', let us know."

Dai now tried to pretend he had actually meant it as a joke but everyone knew he hadn't.

Gwyneth Thomas who owned the café, was next to be acknowledged.

"Well...if for some reason anyone runs out of food due to snow you will always be welcome at my café anytime. I always keep a large stock of food and I also remember the winter of snow from the 1990s. We had a power cut for two days. Well, after that I got a big oven which runs on gas in case the power went off again and I also bought a big industrial microwave so if we have a power cut again I could cook lots of dinners in the oven and put them in the freezer and then when somebody wanted one I could heat them up in the microwave so at least they had a warm meal inside them, and also I won't charge much unless you're an outsider: then you will have to pay 'outsider tax' on it."

"Thank you Gwyneth Thomas, but there is only one thing that concerns me," said the Reverend. "If there's a power cut you won't have any electricity to power your microwave."

"I did not realise that. Well, in that case I could just sell you the dinners and you could take them home and warm them up in your own microwave instead."

Dai looked at the Reverend: "Any thicker and she would be a fridge door".

Mrs Morgan Morgan, who had sat there without saying much at all, now stood up next to the Reverend.

"I would just like to say…"
but before she continued, she looked at the Reverend.

"Sit down. It's my turn to speak."
Like a good little man he obeyed.

"Now, as I was going to say, before you asked about medical treatment, I know I retired a 14-years-and-three-months ago but I still have everything up here," pointing to the side of her head. "I have forgotten more than half of the doctors these days know now. But don't come to me with silly little things like coughs and colds. I will tell you now that if you have them just stay in bed and drink plenty of fluids. If you break something, go to the hospital and if you die: phone the undertakers. Anything else and you can come and see me. I will always be on call 24 hours a day, seven days a week unless *Pobol-y-Cwm* is on or I am in bed sleeping. I hope that is clear to all of you."

The Reverend went to stand up but stopped and looked at Mrs Morgan Morgan first as if to request her permission. Mrs Morgan Morgan gently nodded to him to proceed.

"Well, it seems that there are no really major obstacles to us becoming independent. We have so far confirmed that we will keep the Royal Mail but will change our currency from pounds and pence to Abers and Glas. Also, we will have an assistant for P.C. Williams and also that we are going to have an Army but they won't be 'ass's' anymore. So, anyone wishing to put their name forward for either the police or Army, please let us know by the end of the meeting and we will put your names up outside the hall so people can choose who to vote for. But now there's one more important thing: our new name. We have decided that we should have a vote and everyone will be allowed to vote for our new name, not just people over the age of 18 but also those under that age. Further, we will set up a ballot box at the altar in the chapel and hopefully by Sunday we will have a name that everyone agrees upon. Dai will now give you the options we have come up with but if you do think of your own name for our village, feel free to place that in the box. Now Dai, please will you announce the names that we have chosen?"

"Cheers, Rev. OK folks, these are the ones that we like. First of all we could be 'Commonwealth of Aberglas'; secondly, we could be 'Republic of Aberglas'; the third one we liked was what we are now: 'Aberglas'; and lastly 'Principality of Aberglas'. Now, as the Rev said, anyone with anything different and you are more than welcome to offer your ideas. Back to you Rev."

P.C. Williams rose from his chair at the same time as the Reverend. The latter smiled and acknowledged him.

"First of all," announced P.C. Williams, I would like to thank you for allowing me to have a holiday. I was a bit concerned as I have booked a week away in Devon for a fortnight and would of hated to miss it. But the main problem that concerns me is with the new name choices you have chosen. Firstly, to be a Commonwealth you need either a King or Queen on the throne, and to become a republic you have to let the people govern. Now, if we stay with Aberglas there will be no need to worry. Lastly, for us to become a Principality I believe you need to have a Prince on the throne - but I might be wrong."

The Reverend thanked him and P.C. Williams sat back down.

"Well, it might be better then to stay as 'Aberglas' unless we have a better name to put forward. But I would just like to share this with you: Dai by here thought it would be a good idea to have all four names and become 'Commonwealth Republic Aberglas Principality'. Unfortunately once more he failed to realise that the initials would be 'C', 'R', 'A', 'P'.

The whole crowd burst out laughing; Dai quickly got to his feet.

"I was only joking," although his embarrassment was still perceptible. "Thanks a lot, Rev. You made me look a right div."

"I did not make you a div, boyo: Mother Nature beat me to it."

The laughter died down. The Reverend looked at his watch.

"Well, dearest friends, if there are no more questions or concerns I would like to thank you on behalf of all three of us for attending the meeting. Please don't forget to vote on your favourite name for our new country. You will also need to vote on an assistant for P.C. Williams and lastly, for people to be in our new army, the ones with the most votes will win unless there's a tie for first place. We will then toss an 'Aber' coin!" he laughed.

The meeting was about to adjourn when a voice from the back was heard.

"Are you going to tell us about your trip to Brussels? What you got up to and everything?"

Dai recognised it as Megan's voice.

"I told you, love. It was a diplomatic mission. It was not a jolly-up but if anyone except Megan would like to know anything about the trip, I will be taking questions in the *Drag and Daff* in about half an hour. The Reverend will be there with all the receipts to match the amount of money we spent, as will Mrs Morgan Morgan if you need to seek any medical advice."

"Unfortunately, I will not be able to attend this evening. I have a more important matter to attend to."

She actually had two episodes of *Pobol-y-Cwm* to catch up on video but no-one questioned her.

"Well," said the Reverend, "if there is nothing else, once again thank you, goodnight and God bless."

There were a few claps first of all and then the whole room applauded: "Viva la Revolution!" Everyone then started to make their way either home or to Dai's pub.

The Reverend, Mrs Morgan Morgan and Dai stayed behind as Megan had told Dai that she would open up.

"Well, that went really well! Don't you think so, folks? I don't think anything or anyone can stop us now. This time next month we will be the newest country in the world and won't need to twin with anyone else unless we want to. I personally think it would be a good idea to twin with someone though."

The Reverend and Mrs Morgan Morgan both looked at him in astonishment.

"You really are a div sometimes Dai," declared the Reverend. "The whole reason for becoming independent was because Brynlog wanted us to twin with another place."

"I realise that but now we could choose our own town or place to twin with. Somewhere in Wales would be all right, wouldn't it? At least we could twin with a fellow Welsh town, mun."

"Do you realise Dai, that if and when we become independent we will not be Welsh anymore? I thought I explained that to you already. We will be a different country inside Wales, and not Welsh anymore. We will be just like a lodger in a guesthouse: you will just have to accept that we will no longer be Welsh."

The realisation finally slapped Dai in the face.

"I know you said that but I thought you were just joking, mun? I thought we would be a new country but still remain Welsh...like you would have a map of Wales and then we would be in the middle of it, named 'New Wales' like 'New South Wales' in Australia is?"

"Do you realise that the people in New South Wales are not actually Welsh? They are Australian. They just live in New South Wales," taunted Mrs Morgan Morgan.

"That's what I was trying to say to the both of you. We will be like those in New South Wales in a different country but still be Australian, but we would be Welsh instead of being Australian."

That last statement even confused Dai.

"You know what I mean though."

"It's OK, Dai. I think I know what you mean but it's getting late and don't you have an audience to deal with at the *Drag and Daff*? Let's call it a night, shall we?"

Both agreed and started to make their way out of the hall. Then as Dai switched the light off he quickly switched it back on.

"Dew damm Bach! We forgot one of the most important items!"

The other two stopped in their tracks.

"What is it now?" sighed Mrs Morgan Morgan.

"Flag."

"What did you call me?!" she roared, handbag poised.

"I said 'flag' not 'bag'. We forgot to discuss a new flag for our new country. How could I be so stupid?"

"It's not your fault, Dai. There were a lot of things discussed tonight. One of us was bound to forget something. Don't worry about it."

"You were not stupid tonight for forgetting it."

Her comment actually made Dai smile.

"Thank you."

"No, what I meant to say was, 'you're stupid all the time'."

Mrs Morgan Morgan was just happy that she had got him back for the postage stamp comment. They switched off the light in the hall, locked up and left.

The Reverend and Dai reached the *Drag and Daff* to be greeted by cheers from those already there. Both were really taken aback, obliging Dai to query the welcome.

"Don't get me wrong though, it's nice at last to get a warm welcome when I arrive home!"

Everyone except Megan thought this was funny. Dai quickly realised his mistake and put his arm around her.

"Only joking, love."

Megan pretended to accept his apology but Dai knew she was going to give him such a mouthful when they were alone later. The Reverend meanwhile was shaking people's hands and thanking them all. Then Colin the Cabbie hushed the crowd.

"The reason for the welcome is for what you have done for us. We really appreciate your efforts and everyone is 100% behind you. Aren't we?"

Everyone agreed and started clapping again. Colin moved closer to Dai.

"Could we have a private chat if possible? I need to ask you a personal question."

"Follow me," Dai offered, and they went into the empty lounge area.

"This is my private office. Take a seat, mate. And what can I help you with? I hope though it's not marital problems. I'm no good at those. Look who I married...but if it's not, then fire away, butte. Tell your Uncle Dai all about it."

"Well, it's nothing personal like that. Well...it is a bit but it isn't - if you know what I mean?"

Dai nodded without comprehension.

"Go on."

"The thing is, mate, I have this personal thing that the wife does not know about and I'm hoping you can solve the problem."

"Hang on," Dai interrupted. "Are you sure you don't need to see the Quack about this?"

"It's not medical," laughed Colin. "Listen, the thing is sometimes when the wife thinks I'm working all night, I'm not really."

"Hang on. First of all I know your wife: her name is Linda. There is no need to call her 'the wife' all the time. And secondly, if you're going to admit to having an affair, honest mate, you need to speak to someone else."

Colin once again shook his head.

"The last thing I would do is have an affair, mun. It's not that at all. I could not stand being nagged by two women. I would rather top myself first...

"Now the thing is," he continued, "as I said, once a month I go to Brynlog to meet with a friend and have a good drink and a curry afterwards."

At that point Dai's memory flashed back to his similar but thwarted intentions.

"Then what I do is stay over at a little guesthouse for the night, then drive back home in the morning so it's nothing sinister. The thing is, I pay for this on a credit card that the wi... Linda, I mean, does not know that I have. And once a month when the statement is due to arrive, I have to sit near the front door to wait for Bryn the Post so that I can get to my statement before Linda sees it. You understand what I'm saying, don't you mate?"

"I'm getting there, butte. Now carry on."

"The thing is," Colin continued, "that I owe about £350 on it and what you said earlier in the meeting about changing from pounds to Glas instead made me wonder. If that happens does that mean then I don't owe any money on the credit card now because we have changed currency? Because if that's true, I might get rid of the credit card: too much hassle."

"Well, not as much hassle as having two women on the go at the same time though."

"The thing is," resumed Colin, "I really look forward to my escape once a month. It's great fun meeting with Wilf. He drives taxis as well in Brynlog and we just talk about sport and everything else and what stupid things people say in our cabs. It's a certainty that they always ask, 'Are you busy, drive?' and 'What time you on 'til?' but for one night a month it's so nice not be a husband and a taxi driver, and just be a normal person. And that reminds me: Wilf says he knows you from way back."

Dai looked at Colin.

"What's Wilf's surname? It would not be 'Francis' by any chance, would it?"

"That's right," nodded Colin. "So you *do* know each other, then?"

"Oh yes. I remember Wilf from school. Maybe you should invite him over here one day and we can have a chat about the good old days?"

What this really meant was, yes, Dai could finally get him back for being beaten by him in marbles: "As soon as you try and get through my door you will be banned for life and you will be thrown out so quickly your shadow will still be in the pub whilst you are on your way back home." He smiled at the mere thought of it.

"So Dai, does it mean I don't have to pay my credit card anymore or do I have to sit there for another year or so waiting for Bryn the Post to turn up?"

"I'm sorry, butte. It does not work like that - wish it did though! And anyway, if you only owe just over £300 why don't you pay it off in one go?"

Colin's face was a picture.

"How am I going to explain to Linda that somehow £300 has disappeared from our bank account? All my wages go into it."

"So how do you pay at the moment then if you don't take any money from your bank account?"

"I use the money I get from tips, mun. I usually get about £40-odd quid a month which I use to pay it off with but the interest rates takes half of it so I only ever pay off the bare minimum."

All of a sudden Colin had a brainwave.

"Hang on a minute. I just realised I got another way I could pay it off quicker. If I go to a travel agents maybe I will get a good rate of exchange for my Abers and Glas? I remember my cousin went to America once and got $2 for every £1. Maybe our Glas will be worth 2 British pounds? Then I would only have to pay back 175 Glas instead of £350. I can't believe I did not think of it earlier!"

Dai thought to himself: 'I can't believe that they allow you to drive on public roads'.

"I'm sorry Colin boyo, but we are not officially recognised as having a different currency yet so you will have to keep paying the way you are at the moment."

Colin looked crestfallen so Dai tried to cheer him up.

"Don't worry mate! Maybe in a couple of weeks when we are recognised as an independent country and with our own currency, then you will get a good rate of exchange. You don't mind waiting a couple of weeks more, do you butte?"

"I don't mind at all, mate. But can we keep this meeting amongst the two of us only?"

Dai lifted up his thumb, turned his hand upside down and placed the upside-down thumb on his forehead: "Husbands' honour. Now let's get back to the bar. I got a mouth like a sandfly's armpit."

The bar was still quite full of excited chatter. Dai poured himself a pint and then stood there like a lord surveying his land, nodding now and again to people who lifted up their pint to him. Megan noticed this and punched him gently on his arm, making him spill some of his lager.

"What the hell is wrong with you, woman?" Dai shrieked.

"I just wanted to check you were still with us. You looked as if you were lording it over everyone."

"Don't be stupid, love," and then to himself, "How the hell does she know what I'm thinking all the time?"

Returning to Megan, Dai proclaimed his pleasure in having everyone on their side. Megan smiled and went to rub Dai's arm where she had hit him. Dai automatically flinched and pulled it away, thinking she was going to punch him again - and consequently spilt some more of his lager on the floor.

"I think you got a drink problem, Dai."

"What do you mean, love?"

"Well, you keep spilling it over the floor."

"Well, if you stopped hitting my arm, it would stay in the glass instead of on the floor. I think I had better make it safe."

In one quick gulp Dai sank the remaining three quarters of his pint. He poured himself another and then placed his two hands tightly around the glass, moving around Megan to the other side of the bar thinking that it would be safer away from her reach.

Chatting idly to some of the locals, Dai was interrupted by his own train of thought.

"My friends, listen! I have something important to say."

The crowd quietened.

"The thing is I forgot to mention the flag. We will need a new flag for our new country."

Dai looked around the bar for Mrs Griffiths, the local primary school teacher.

"Mrs Griffiths. Could you ask the children to design a new flag in your art class and then the best one will win some sweets up to the value of 1 Glas, from Sian's shop? I will personally pay for the prize out of my own pocket."

"You tight bugger!" piped Megan. "Dai will pay the winner 5 Glas from his own pocket: I can guarantee that."

Dai tried to protest that giving out that many sweets would be bad for the children's teeth, hoping everyone would agree with him. Colin tried to defend Dai but it backfired on the two of them when, to Dai's immense shock, Megan also agreed with them.

"The thing is, you're both right. That was a bit stupid of me to say. So instead of giving 5 Glas to buy sweets and also to save the children's teeth, Dai will give a 10-Glas gift voucher for the toy shop in Brynlog instead."

Unfortunately for Dai she announced this just as he was taking a sip of his pint. He not only nearly choked on it but once again spilt some of his lager on the floor. Megan tried not to laugh.

"That's really generous of you, Dai. Don't you agree everyone?"

It met with rapturous approval.

During the following days all people talked about was their new independence: how they would be a lot better off no longer belonging to the United Kingdom and that before long they would have their own rugby team good enough to take on the world. They would even be as good as Wales one day; according to some they were even better than England already.

The shops were already advertising their imminent acceptance of Abers and Glas, with British currency soon to be declined but the truth was that they would still be using British currency: only the names would be changed. But if you asked anyone in the village it was still a new currency. Sian the Shop had gone one better and spent nearly ten hours removing the original prices off all her items, replacing them 'Gs' instead of '£s', or 'As' instead of a 'pence' sign. She was very proud of her hard work until someone asked her what would happen if they were not allowed to change currency?

She would presumably have to take all the stickers back off and replace them again? Sian's face was a picture but she maintained that even if the currency could not be changed, she would still use Abers and Glas until all the stock with the new prices had been sold. Then she would revert to pounds and pence. There was no way she was going to replace all the stickers.

Meanwhile Mrs Griffiths' primary school class was busy designing a new flag for their new country. It seemed that the most popular designs did not consist of dragons or daffodils but instead of dinosaurs and flying saucers. Nonetheless, every single design would be judged on merit in the village hall and the best two would be voted on by everyone in the chapel on the Sunday. Here the winner would receive the gift voucher generously donated by Dai the Pub - who was still in a mood with Megan for offering it.

"Do you think I'm made of money?"

"If you were, I would chop your head off as I have seen a nice dress in Brynlog," replied his wife - which did nothing to quell his anger.

The rest of the village walked around with big smiles on their faces and excited glints in their eyes. They had never had this much excitement since the infamous funeral of Mr Thomas.

The Reverend, Mrs Morgan Morgan and Dai had decided not to meet up until the Friday at the village hall so that they would not be influenced by each other's ideas: it seemed the fairest way. They would be like everyone else and see the ideas for the new flags all at the same time. The only people who knew what the new flags looked like were the children and Mrs Griffiths, and she would be the one who would mount the drawings in the village hall after school on the Friday, ready for their village judgement. None of the drawings would be named in order to stop relatives voting for their child's masterpiece. Only Mrs Griffith's knew the identities, having committed them to an exercise book now safely locked away in her desk drawer. Finally, just to ensure complete fairness, none of the children would be allowed in the village hall until everyone had voted for their choice.

The Reverend had visited the school just before the competition had begun. Gently he told the children that if any one of them described their designs to their parents, that it would not only be very naughty but also would make all the angels cry. To seal the deal, he also told them that they would all burn in Hell and their toys be melted down there along with them. This was rather excessive from the Reverend, making a lot of the children cry – and some for the first time in many years. The Reverend had no choice but to apologise, claiming that he was only pretending: just their toys would be melted down.

The final two drawings would be selected by Mrs Griffith's before being presented in the chapel on Sunday so that everyone could see how their new flag would really look before their final vote was cast by a show of hands from the congregation.

Once the best one had been chosen, Colin the Cabbie would drive down to Swansea to a place he knew that made flags for ships. He would bring back the official flag later in the day.

The other pressing matter that needed resolution on Sunday was their new name. Some of the locals did not want any change but as Dai said on the Thursday night in the pub, 'What's the point of a new currency and a new flag and still have the old name? It's the way forward. It's the best thing for Aberglas. Megan countered with 'It's not the best thing for Aberglas as after Sunday Aberglas will no longer exist anymore'. This made the whole pub fall silent: it was all well and good going independent but nobody realised that it could mean the end of Aberglas. It would no longer exist - which actually brought tears to Dai's eyes. He quickly wiped them away but not before Megan noticed and put her arm around him.

"You all right, Dai? You look like you're crying."

"Don't be stupid, love. I'm not a Babi-lol. I just got something in my eye, that's all."

"It's a tear, Dai," she whispered, and gently kissed him on his cheek. For the first time in ages Megan had actually showed him some affection in public; Dai turned and smiled at her. Gwyneth Jones then spoke.

"I would like to propose a toast," raising her glass, "to Aberglas no longer here but forever in our hearts" - which promptly fetched a tear to everyone's elses eyes in the pub.

"Well, on Monday we will be a new country with a new flag and a new name. And just to remind you all, we will also have a new currency so if any of you want to get rid of your old pounds and pence before then I am quite willing to exchange them for alcohol!"
Everyone fell about laughing.

"What they laughing at? I'm being deadly serious here."

"I tell you something, Dai," smiled Megan taking his hand, "everything around us is going to change but you will never change. You will always be as tight as a duck's bum."

Friday evening finally arrived. Everyone in the village had turned up outside the hall at 6pm waiting for Mrs Griffiths to allow them inside so that they could choose their new flag. Yet as there were over 500 people outside and the village hall could only accommodate about 200, there would be only 100 allowed in at one time. These would be given 20 minutes to look at the drawings and then vote in the box provided by the door. As there were only 25 entries, this would give people plenty of time. The whole event would be over by about 7.30pm.

This gave Dai the idea of holding a 'Farewell to the old Welsh flag' night at the pub. He would invite everyone to bring in their old Welsh flags and then put them in a box to be buried at the back of the beer garden - like some sort of funeral to the old country. Megan was right: any excuse to make people come to the pub and spend their money. It was one of the things that attracted her to him in the first place although she did sometimes think that he was too tight with his finances. She often said that the Queen had to put sunglasses on when Dai opened his wallet in case the light hurt her eyes.

Sunday's chapel was full to capacity: this was not going to be a normal Sunday sermon. This was going to go down in history as the first one for the new country and the last one for Aberglas.

The Reverend Emmanuel stood in his pulpit and commenced the sermon in his powerful voice - the one he kept only for a Sunday.

"Today is a funeral and also a birth. It is the funeral of old Aberglas and the birth of our new country."

Those villagers who thought this was going to be a different, more relaxed sermon soon realised their error.

"The birth," he continued, "of a new country is exciting and although this is a fresh start for all of us, the sins you committed whilst living in Aberglas and indeed Wales will follow you into this new country of ours. So don't think you have got away with anything."

At this point the Reverend looked around the chapel. Colin the Cabbie ducked to avoid his gaze. Linda noticed this and whispered to Colin: "If you got something to confess, love..." Luckily Colin thought quickly: "Just checking my flies done up, love. Felt a bit of a breeze then" and smiled innocently at her. He was in the right place, praying so hard inside that she actually believed him.

The chapel service ended. Usually this would prompt a charge for the doors, the Reverend having condemned them all to Hell at least four times during his sermon. Yet today was different: first of all nobody moved and secondly the Reverend had only condemned them to Hell twice: he must be in a good mood, most of them thought. He then invited Mrs Morgan Morgan and Dai to join him at the altar as they were the three that had gone over to a far-flung land, as Dai had told everyone. So it only seemed fair that they were at the front of the chapel for the momentous occasion.

"First of all, I would like to thank you all for coming." The Reverend tapped Dai on his shoulder, obliging Dai to move towards him.

"First of all, Dai, it's not a birthday party. You do not thank people for coming to chapel. It is for their own good otherwise how would they know how to get to Hell and secondly, this is a house of God and I'm the tenant. So I suggest you step back and shut up. You already know you're going to Hell but if you want to get there sooner, carry on! Otherwise I suggest you take a back seat and let me do the talking."

Mrs Morgan Morgan, who had been very quiet whilst this was going on, grabbed the piece of typed paper from the Reverend's hand.

"I will make both of your lives a living Hell if you two don't shut up!"

She then walked up three steps to the pulpit from where the Reverend usually conducted his sermons.

"First of all, there were four main issues we needed to vote on and here are the first three results."

Colin the Cabbie lent forward in anticipation. He had been the only one going around the village trying to get people to vote for him as he saw it as the biggest money-making idea he had ever had.

"The person who will assist P.C. Williams in his duties," she continued, "will be…Mrs Griffiths', the primary school teacher's husband, Thomas Griffiths."

This was met with a large round of applause. The reason for the choice was that Thomas Griffiths had childlocks on his car doors so that the criminal could not escape on his way to prison.

"So, well done Thomas Griffiths!"

Colin the cabbie folded his arms in disgust: "That should have been me," he moaned to Linda.

"The reason I think you lost," she argued, "was you saying that if you had to take prisoners anywhere you would put the taxi meter on. I think that might have gone against you."

"The second vote for responsibility for transportation in extreme weather," continued Mrs Morgan Morgan, "well, that position goes to…"

Once again Colin lent forward.

"…Hywel Thomas. He has just had a new four-wheel drive People-Carrier delivered, so well done!"

"I don't believe this," cried Colin. "This is so unfair!"

Linda put her hand on Colin's.

"Did you say something about putting the meter on again?" she asked gently.

Colin just nodded.

"You are such a div, sometimes."

"And now the time has come to announce the new name for our new country. It was a very close result but one name came out on top, and that name is...."

Mrs Morgan Morgan paused for dramatic effect here. Considering that she was always known for her bluntness and straight-talking, she seemed to enjoy the suspense she was creating.

"The new name for our new country is: 'New Aberglas of New Wales'."

Everyone cheered at the name. Mrs Morgan Morgan put her hand up to hush the crowd.

"The runner-up was 'Aberglas Sovereign State' but I think it was noticed that the initials would have been 'A.S.S.' Personally, I believe that this was just a silly prank and the people who voted for it are indeed 'arses' - to which everyone burst out laughing.

Mrs Morgan Morgan then gestured Mrs Griffiths to the altar. Once the laughter had subsided, she recommenced.

"Now, we have two choices of flags to vote on, and Mrs Griffiths has copied them to a better standard than the original ones, so please show the first one."

Mrs Griffiths duly lifted up the first, it was a cuddley looking dragon, then the second which was a fire breathing dragon

"The vote is now open. Can I see a show of hands for the first one?"

About half the congregation raised their hands.

"Now, can I see a show of hands for the second one, please?"

It seemed that the other half put up their hands. Mrs Morgan Morgan noticed that Mrs Tompkins, sitting in the front row, had raised her hand for both of them.

"You can't vote for them both!"

"Well, we can't have one side of the flag with the first one and the other side of the flag with the second one!"

Dai the Pub approached.

"Can I just say something? The first one is cute and cuddly and seems to say 'Come on in, we are open' but the second one seems to say 'Don't mess with us!' Which do we want? I vote Number Two. Anyone with me?"

With that, nearly all of them put up their hands.

"You should have let me do the talking. I know what the people want."

Mrs Morgan Morgan chose to ignore him.

"Well, it's decided then. Our new flag is the second one. Colin the Taxi Driver, you have a very important mission. Can you take the winning one to Swansea and have it made up into our official flag?"

"Oh, so they want me now do they?" he said to Linda. "Well I don't think I can be bothered to drive down to Swansea."

"Oh don't be such a big babi-lol," retorted his wife.

The Reverend decided to follow Dai's lead and move to the front of the altar.

"Well, my friends. This has been a monumental day in the history of New Aberglas. Now I would like to be the first person to welcome you all to our new country, 'New Aberglas in New Wales'. The only two things we need to do now are to find a new national anthem and also to notify the Welsh government that we no longer belong to them." Looking at Mrs Griffiths, he continued,

"I know you are not only the art teacher but you are the music teacher as well. So, would it be possible if you could write a new national anthem for us?"

Dai piped up, "I can do that, mun. I'm good at limericks and I know a load of old rugby songs. We could just change the words so the music will already be written for it."

"I think it would be better if we let Mrs Griffiths do it," insisted the Reverend. "We don't want a new national anthem with lots of swearing in it!"

"If Dai wants to help," interjected Mrs Griffiths, "I will be grateful."

"She knows talent when she sees it. We will be the new Rodgers and Hammerstein, won't we?"

"Well, let's hope so, Dai."

The Reverend turned to the congregation.

"Once again before you all leave, I would like to thank Mrs Morgan Morgan for the announcements. You may come down now…and don't worry: normal service will be resumed next week!"

The Reverend laughed at his own joke.

"Also I would like to thank Mrs Griffiths for the drawings and lastly, thanks to all of you for being here for the dawn of a new country."

As he uttered those words, the heavens opened and the rain belted down.

Dai smiled: "We may be a 'New Wales' but at least it will still rain. Reminds me a bit of the old Wales."

Chapter Nine

Casualties of war

Two days later Dai was sitting in the bar before opening time, humming a tune to himself whilst he chewed on his pencil. On the table in front of him was a pile of blank paper; on the floor were the rolled-up scraps.

"How hard is it to write a national anthem?" he asked Megan who was sitting on her bar stool having a cuppa and reading the morning paper.

"Why can't we just have a limerick instead? I'm really good at those. I can make them up in ten minutes or so but writing a national anthem is hard. I think people should realise I'm not a composer like that fellow Bach was. I just wish he was here at the moment to help out a fellow Welsh man."

Megan looked up from her paper.

"Bach was not Welsh. He was German, you div! His Christian names were 'Johannes Sebastian'."

"Hang on. He was German? Are you sure, love? I think you might be wrong as I know a Joanne and a Sebastian and they were born up the road, not in Germany. Are you sure you're right, love?"

Megan shook her head in disbelief.

"Let me tell you that when I was in school we learnt about composers and the one I liked the most was Bach, so I'm 110% right!"

"Did you go to school with him, then?"

Dai loved to rub in the fact that Megan was four years older than him. Megan might have learnt about Bach in school but Dai had learnt how to wind Megan up - and also when to duck as Megan threw a wet cloth in his direction.

"How come then, that his name is Bach and he is German? 'Bach' is Welsh for 'boy', for goodness sake!"

"I know what 'Bach' means, you sledge! [idiot]. And you also know I speak better Welsh than you."

"But not as good as English as what I is!" he replied, bursting out laughing. "I just wish though that it was as easy to write a national anthem as it is to make people laugh."

"I don't think you realise, Dai, that the person who finds your jokes the funniest most of the time, is you."

"Well, as long as somebody does, I don't mind."

Megan left her stool and walked towards Dai.

"What are you trying to say in the anthem? Maybe I can help you out?"

She picked up one of the scraps of paper on the floor, unravelled it and looked at what Dai had written:

'*Oh Aberglas now that you're gone,
New Aberglas has just begon
We live in the country of new Wales now
But we still got six sheep to every cow.*'

This time it was Megan's turn to burst out laughing.

"Well, for a start there is no such word as 'begon': it's 'begun'."

"I know that but 'begun' does not rhyme. 'Begon' does! All songs need to rhyme. You should have learnt that when you were in school with old boy Bach!"

"Do you want my help or not?" snapped Megan. "Otherwise you can just sit there and carry on wasting your time!"

The trouble with Dai was, that like many husbands he would never ask Megan for help outright. Instead he would say something like, 'If you think you can do better, be my guest', and 'The trouble is, all wives know that men are asking for their help but pretend they don't know, to spare their husbands' feelings'. But Megan was not your typical wife.

"So you *do* need my help!"

"I did not say I needed your help, did I? The trouble with you, Megan, is that you always twist things around to your way of thinking. Over the years I have noticed that about you. I think you should remember, Megan love, who is the man and therefore the head of the household."

"I know who the man is, and you are indeed the head of the household when I'm not here. But as I am here now you are second-in-command. But don't worry. I'm out tomorrow so you can be in charge for a couple of hours. Now stop wingeing and let's get a start on this anthem of yours."

The Reverend and Mrs Morgan Morgan were sitting in his kitchen, also with a notepad and pencil on the table. Mrs Morgan Morgan had decided that it would be in the best interest of the village if just he and she were responsible for drafting the official letter to the Welsh government explaining their new independence. Well, her exact words were: "If David the Public House has anything to do with writing the letter, it will just be another cheap publicity stunt for his Public House - like the shameless way he advertised it on the plane when he was walking up and down the aisle."

"You have got to give him his due though," laughed the Reverend. "He might be slightly annoying but he's got a good head for business: there was no way anyone could not have noticed his walking advertisement there!"

"*Slightly* annoying? It's more than 'slightly'! He is immensely annoying. You may think he is funny but I do not. Am I the only one in this village who sees the man for what he really is?"

"Can you explain then, who the real Dai is?" goaded the Reverend.

"We don't have time to go through all his faults now as *Pobol-Y-Cwm* is on in ten hours and I want to be home to watch it! Now let's get back to the business of writing this letter. I know I was against the idea at the beginning but after the meeting and the way everyone backed you and David the Public House, it actually swayed me to agree with the pair of you."

As she said this she actually looked a little emotional.

"Is that your way of actually saying you agree with Dai the Pub? Well, in all my life I never thought I would see the day when you did this!"

"Well, if you ever tell David the Public House that I thought he was right, it will be your last day on earth. Do I make myself clear, Reverend Ivor Emmanuel?"

Use of his full name convinced the Reverend as to her sincerity and he quickly decided to change the subject.

Unfortunately, he made the fatal mistake of speaking without thinking first.

"Have you ever thought of being nice to people for a change? It would make their lives and yours a much happier one."

"I will have you know that I used to be very nice and loving, but the three men I loved all died and left me! When Mr Morgan passed - God rest his soul - I decided then that no-one was ever going to hurt me again."

As she said this her eyes glazed over. In that moment the Reverend realised that inside her there was indeed a loving lady but that Mrs Morgan Morgan had locked her deep away. He therefore quickly resolved to change the subject.

"Well, as you said, your favourite programme is on in ten hours so we had better get this letter written!"

Mrs Morgan Morgan took a deep breath to compose herself.

"Oh, good. You have finally remembered why we are here, then? Enough of this idle chat."

Mrs Morgan Morgan picked up the pencil off the table.

"Now: I will be the one to write it down as all you men have terrible writing. If cave women had drawn on their cave walls instead of the cave men, archeologists would have had no problem in understanding what they were. Not only would the drawings have been better but the cave women would also have written an explanation underneath. So, do you have any objection to my writing this?"

Before the Reverend could open his mouth, Mrs Morgan Morgan said, "Good. I'm glad you agree. Now let's get started."

Just over an hour later, and with a bit of tweaking, the letter was written, ready for posting to the Welsh government:

'New Aberglas New Wales
No postcode yet

To the person in charge of Welsh matters,
We are writing to inform you that we are no longer going to be part of Wales or the United

Kingdom. This is partly due to our opposition against the proposal of being twinned with a village in a different country and also the way we were threatened with arrest by a certain councillor after we had politely requested him to reconsider the proposal.

We would also like to inform you that we have been on a fact-finding mission to Europe to ensure we are allowed to become independent and now also have the backing of a European delegate, which we will refuse to name in case you try to change his mind.

We have further decided to change our currency from pounds and pence to Abers and Glas, and we are hoping that in a couple of weeks that this will be recognised as an official currency.

The next point we would like to tell you about is that we now have a new national anthem which we also believe will be accepted worldwide.

Fourthly, we have decided upon a new flag for our new nation, which we will fly proudly above our town hall and also should be recognised as a new addition to the world's flags.

Fifthly, after careful consideration and public voting, we have increased our police force. In fact we have now double the amount of police officers we had previously. We understand that each country around the world, whether friendly or hostile, requires and needs armed forces and we were considering bringing back national service. But before that was put to the public vote we had an influx of volunteers which now means that we are fully prepared for any circumstances.

However, one thing concerns us, and we are hoping you will consider our proposal: that until we are able to purchase our own fire engine, could we hire one off you, if you have any spare ones - for a nominal fee, of course?

Lastly, we wish to inform you that we will still be using our old United Kingdom passports until we

can get the official new Aberglas ones. We would like to thank you for allowing us to be part of Wales for such a long time but from now on we will no longer be so but if you do wish to discuss any of these points further, please reply to our address at the top of the letter – and we wish you good luck for your future.
  Yours sincerely,
  On behalf of all-new Aberglas,

  Mrs Morgan Morgan

  The Reverend read the letter in disbelief.
  "You seem to have exaggerated somewhat with a couple of the facts, if you don't mind me pointing them out to you, Mrs Morgan Morgan?"
  "And *what* precisely may they be, then?" she glowered.
  "Well, first of all you state that we have doubled our police force, and secondly that we have had an influx of volunteers for our armed forces."
  "That, for a start, is not an exaggeration. We *have* doubled our police force, haven't we? Before there was only P.C. Williams but now we also have Mr Griffiths. Secondly, my Great-great-great nephews on the late Mr Morgan's side are in the Army Cadets and I'm sure I could persuade them and their friends to help us out if we ever have to go to war. Remember, blood is thicker than water - and also I send them £10 every year at Christmas, so if they did not come to our aid I would stop sending them the money."
  "Fair enough. In that case I retract my statement and apologise profusely to you."
  "You're not in chapel now. It's just us two, so there is no need to speak as if you had swallowed a dictionary. Say what you mean, man!"
  "Well, in that case, I'm sorry I called you a liar. But you should have let me know about your Great-great-great nephews being in the Army Cadets before I questioned it."
  Mrs Morgan Morgan growled at him before rolling into a talking frenzy:

"Do you expect me to tell you everything about myself or what I do? I suppose you will now want me to phone you every time I go to do something, just so that I don't have secrets from you! Is that what you want? Well, let me tell you: that will never happen, you understand me?"

"I did not mean it that way. But it would have just been nice of you to have explained this to me before I read the letter. It then would have saved this pointless argument - that's all I'm trying to say."

"Well, I have wasted enough time here," she announced, looking at her watch. "I will take the letter and give it to Mrs Griffiths, the primary school teacher, to type up ready to send to Cardiff and also to London. And before you say it, I will ask her to do two copies: one for each office in case you thought I was going to ask the Cardiff office to send it to London after they had finished reading it."

Mrs Morgan Morgan picked up her handbag and folded the letter. She then buttoned up her coat and straightened her hat.

"I will show myself out, and will inform you when the letter has been sent. Good morning to you, Reverend."
With that she marched out of the kitchen.

"Well, Ivor," exclaimed the Reverend to himself, "for one moment there she was nearly human like the rest of us."
He then raised his eyes and prayed out loud:

"Dear Lord, I would just like to warn You that You are going to have Your hands full when she gets up there with You. And please don't take this the wrong way but I can now understand why Dai will be happy going down instead of up. But if I could ask You a small favour...would it be possible to place Mrs Morgan Morgan in her own special private part in the Kingdom of Heaven, as I would be very grateful - and I assume the others up there will be too? Amen."

Meanwhile Megan and Dai were still sitting in the bar working on a new national anthem. They remained unaware of the meeting that had taken place between the Reverend and Mrs Morgan Morgan. Suddenly the phone behind the bar rang. Megan answered. It was Colin.

"Hello Colin. What is it I can do for you?"

Megan proceeded to nod, as if Colin could see her, and sound like a parrot. Every so often she would say "I see," "uh huh," "I see," and "uh huh." After a couple of minutes she put the phone down and returned to Dai.

"So, what did Colin want, my love? Is everything OK with the flag?"

"I think so but I got a bit confused with what he said."

"Well, what did he say, then?"

"Well, Colin might have to wait 'til Thursday for the flag as his friend the flag maker is not only very busy but he is also in plaster. At least I think that's what Colin said."

Dai shook his head.

"Oh, that's just great! If it's his arm in plaster he won't be able to do it. Unless someone else can, we won't have a new flag for ages."

"Don't panic quite yet. Colin did not say whether it was the arm or leg, and as he is on his way home we will know later."

"Well in that case, it's back to the drawing board. Come on, our new country needs a new national anthem and if we write it we will be remembered as the ones who did it!"

Dai once again looked at the blank piece of paper, and then at Megan.

"Well, if a foreigner can write a national anthem surely a Welshman can. We are all born with a song in our heart and music in our blood. But what we need firstly though is to have a cuppa: I will have two sugars in mine, love."

"Well then. It's a good job you're going to make it then! And while you're there, I will have two sweeteners in mine. Thanks, my love."

Dai shook his head in resignation. When he returned from the kitchen, Megan had already put on the stereo from behind the bar. Classical music now played in the background. Dai placed the coffees on the table, looked up at Megan, and then down at the stereo before staring back at his wife.

"Why have you put that on? It's going to be distracting. You need peace and quiet to write music. I bet Rodgers and Hammerstein didn't have Radio Classic on when they wrote *The Sound of Music*, otherwise it would not have been *'How do you solve a problem like Maria?'* but rather *'How do you compose a song like Mozart?"*

"It's for inspiration, you sledge! I'm trying to pick a tune that we can use and then put words to it."

The next tune started playing. It was *O Fortuna*, the theme tune from *The Exorcist* as well as the tune that played on Mrs Morgan Morgan's door bell. It seemed to be haunting Dai, provoking a cold shiver down his back.

"There is no way we are going to use that tune! It's enough to scare the heebie-jeebies out of you! Can't we just nick a national anthem off another country and change the words? It would be a lot easier. I could have it written in about twenty minutes then."

"OK Mr Composer," challenged Megan, looking at her watch, "try putting new words to *God Save the Queen* and I will be back in 20 minutes to hear this great and wondrous anthem!"

"Right," thought Dai thought to himself. "Let's prove that witch wrong. "OK, wake up brain," he commanded, tapping his forehead: "It's time to go to work."

It was indeed 20 minutes later when Megan returned to the bar.

"Well, Mr Composer? Have you created the masterpiece?"

"Yes, my little nest of vipers - and it's a sure winner! I bet you thought I did not have it in me. Well, guess what? I have! And it was so easy. I'm thinking of writing a musical next."

"OK," laughed Megan. "Let's hear it."

Dai stood up and took a deep breath.

"We are New Aberglas
We are surrounded by green green grass
In New Aberglas
It's the nicest place you see
Not far from Swansea
You're welcome to have a cup of tea
In New Aberglas

*You can pop in any time
Our weather's always fine
The Drag and Daff serves food til 9
In New Aberglas."*

Dai took a bow. "Thank you, thank you. See? I told you it was easy!"

Megan's face was a mixture of shock and disbelief.

"Do you really honestly think people are going to accept that as our new national anthem?"

"What's wrong with it? It's perfect. It's bound to be picked! What's wrong with it?"

"There is only one thing wrong with it, my love. 'The weather's always fine'? What the hell are you talking about? It did not rain as much after Noah had built his ark as it does here! We are the only place in the world where wellies are compulsory - but I did like the bit about us serving food 'til nine. I will give you that."

"That's just your opinion, love. I will put it to the public vote and then when everyone agrees with me that it's the greatest anthem ever written, you will eat your words."

"Well, if it is accepted as our new national anthem, Dai, I will give you what you always wanted - and I have always refused to!"

Dai's eyes lit up.

"Yes. I will make you a curry."

"Well that's even better than what I was thinking!"

The clock chimed eleven.

"Well, time to let my adoring fans in," beamed Dai, making his way towards the door.

"Good morning, Bryn. You finished your round early today! If your boss knows you're in here so early…you will get the sack!"

He pointed at the postal sack on Bryn's shoulder.

"Sorry! Guess you already had the sack!"

"Well, I never heard that one before," replied Bryn. "I'm actually not here for a drink. I'm here to ask what our new postcode is going to be so that I can let my bosses know. Otherwise you might not get any letters."

"Well, no letters means no bills either, so that sounds like a good plan! Actually at the moment Bryn, we don't have a new postcode but as soon as we do you will be the second to know."

"So who is going to be the first one to know it then?"

"Me, of course, you div! Otherwise I would not know it to tell you, would I?"

"Um, OK. I think, well...I must get on. See you tonight."

At this point Colin the Cabbie pulled up outside the *Dragon and Daff*.

"How is your mate, butte? Was it his arm or leg - and will he still be able to do it for us?"

Colin's face was as blank as Bryn the Postie's had been.

"What you talking about Dai, mun? Is you lost the plot?"

"No, I'm functioning fully, thank you. I'm on about what you said about your mate when you phoned earlier and told Megan that your mate was in plaster. I'm just a bit concerned, that's all."

"What the hell do you mean, Dai? There's nothing wrong with him – well, there wasn't when I left him - it's just he has a lot on at the moment due to a big order for flags for the Regatta next week."

"You stupid sledge," Dai shouted across to his wife, now entertaining a couple of friends. "He's not in plaster, he's busy with flags for a 'regatta'."

Incensed, Megan left her stool.

"Listen, you two. First of all, David, don't you ever call me a 'div' in front of my friends again, and also, Colin, you need to learn to pronounce your words better. Don't you know how to speak the Queen's English? Honest: some people doesn't know how to talk proper."

With that she headed back to where her friends were sitting.

"I didn't call her a 'div': I called her a 'sledge'." Then, turning to Colin, "You no doubt told her it was a 'Regatta'? Maybe it's Megan's ears that doesn't understand the Queen's English?"

With this, they both roared out laughing but stopped when they caught her evil stare.

"Well, that's it," said Colin. I'm off before she comes back over."

"Thanks mate," smiled Dai, patting him on the shoulder, "I now know how the captain feels when the rats start leaving a sinking ship."

"Don't worry: I'm with you in spirit, Dai."

Next the Reverend entered the pub.

"Morning Rev! Run out of holy water have you? I can sell you a bottle of still water if you want one or are you after something stronger?"

"Morning, Dai. I'm not here for a drink actually - and if I were in your shoes I would try and keep as much water as possible: you are going to need it to put out the fires of Hell when you get there! I have only come here to tell you that we have written two letters to the Welsh government: one for the Cardiff office and one for the London office."

"You wrote them behind my back," complained Dai crestfallen. "What's the matter? Were you afraid I would not be able to use big words? I will have you know I'm highly electrocuted, er…I mean 'educated'. Just because I'm an ex-rugby player does not mean I don't have it upstairs. Never suffered any brain injury up here: I'm as sharp as Megan's tongue," he finished, pointing at his head.

The Reverend tried to spare Dai's feelings.

"No Dai. It's nothing like that. I know you have intellect. It's just that we did not want to burden you with the trivial task of writing a letter as we assumed you would be busy composing our new national anthem. How's it going by the way?"

"Done and done," proclaimed Dai puffing out his chest. "I'm thinking of writing a musical next. It's so easy to write songs. I could be in London next year, with my musical being the top one to see."

Megan had by now made her way up to the pair of them. She laughed at Dai's last statement.

"The only way you will be in London next year is if we go on a day trip, you div!"

"I bet that boy Bach did not have a woman laughing at him when he was composing!"

"Do you mean the composer Bach?" enquired the Reverend. "If so, I don't think he was actually married. But then again he might have been. Don't take my word for it."

"See?" said Dai. "Not only was he a great composer but highly intelligent too: managing to avoid getting married he must have died a happy man."

Instinctively Dai swerved to avoid Megan's jab.

"Anyway," resumed the Reverend, "why I came here was just to let you know what was happening. Mrs Morgan Morgan took the letter to Mrs Griffiths to type up and then post. So hopefully they will have it either tomorrow or the day after. Then I'm hoping that by the weekend we will be recognised as a new independent country."

"Oh, I see the anti-Christ of Aberglas wrote the letter. No wonder I was not invited. Now, be honest with me Rev - and remember you're a man of the cloth so you can't lie - do you think Mrs Morgan Morgan doesn't love me anymore?"

The Reverend pulled out from his pocket the little Bible he always carried with him. He placed his hand upon it.

"To be honest with you, you're not that special. I think she does not love anyone apart from her cat and *Pobol-Y-Cwm*. Anyway, back to the national anthem. You said you had finished it. May I see it, please?"

"I can do better than that. I will sing it for you."

Dai started singing it at full pelt. As he did so, the Reverend's eyes widened in disbelief. At its conclusion, the Reverend just nodded as he did not want to upset him twice in the space of ten minutes.

"Well that's certainly going to take some beating, that's for sure," while privately thinking to himself, "Please Lord, let Mrs Griffith's pen a better one. It cannot be any worse than the one Dai has just sung to me."

"Well Dai," he outwardly resumed, "that must have taken you a long time to compose?"

"You must be joking, mun. It only took me about ten minutes or so. I reckon I could write a musical in an afternoon. I have already got a story for my musical: it's about a publican that murders his wife and buries her in his cellar. The main song has already been written and better still it is also the same title as the musical. It's called 'Happy Days are here again'."

Dai thought that he was still out of Megan's reach. Unfortunately, she had actually moved closer to him – to administer a sharp pain down his right shin. Dai yelped, lifted his leg up and started rubbing his shin.

"You stupid sledge! You could have warned me you were going to do that!"

"I did not want to spoil the surprise, Dai. I know how much you like surprises."

The Reverend pretended to look at his watch.

"Oh well. I must be off. Got to visit Mrs Davies. She's had a family bereavement and I'm going to try to console her." Dai and Megan both looked at him.

"Is that Miss Williams that was?" enquired Megan. "If it is I did not know someone had died. But don't worry though: we will organise a whip-round for some flowers. Who died, may I ask?"

"There will be no need for flowers," smiled the Reverend, "although it was a lovely thought. The person was not actually a living person who died: it was her parrot."

"Hang on a minute," interrupted Dai. "I have never understood that statement. How can a living person be dead? It makes no sense to me."

"Sometimes love you're so tup. A person has to be living to be dead. You can't have a dead person dead or a dead person living – unless, of course, it's a zombie and everyone knows that zombies don't exist. And I don't think anyone would be that tup to believe zombies did exist!"

Megan smiled as she knew she had hit upon Dai's only real fear: zombies. Apparently when Dai was about five his mother had taken him shopping to Cardiff for the day. As they passed a clothes' shop she had stopped to look at the dresses in the window. Dai stared at the mannequins, when all of a sudden one of them moved. Unbeknown to Dai it was actually only one of the shop assistants who had just finished dressing one of the mannequins and had stopped to check that everything was in order. But this had not stopped Dai from belting down the road crying, his mother chasing after him. When his mother finally caught up, she tried explaining what had really happened. However, even to this day Dai could not look at a mannequin. Deep within his unconscious self Dai still believed that mannequins were really zombies in disguise. The *Dragon and Daff* every year held a Halloween party for the village kids and the only rule was that under no circumstances could anyone dress up as a zombie. Witches and ghosts were OK but zombies could actually scare the younger children attending the party. The villagers therefore thought Dai was very considerate in doing this, although little did they know that it was borne out of sheer self-interest.

    This time it was Dai who threw Megan the evil stare: she would be the one buried next door to the witch.

    "Are you OK, Dai?" asked the Reverend. "You have gone a little pale."

    "I'm fine, Rev. It's just I don't like talk of zombies in the pub in case there may be a child in here. I don't want to scare them as it's not even Halloween."

    "Do you know, Dai, you should have become a Reverend like me?" placing his hand on Dai's shoulder. "I have never known anyone care so much for the children that was not a man of the cloth, let alone a publican! You really are a gentle giant."

    "Don't think Dai could have done your job," smirked Megan. "Not very keen on death or dying, are you love?"

    At this moment Dai thought how much it would have been a pleasure to have laid his wife to rest, "you evil witch". Instead, he merely replied,

    "No, love. I prefer to get them plastered not cremated."

    "Well, don't get them too plastered," laughed the Reverend. "I heard a story once that an alcoholic who passed away took three days to turn to ashes: the alcohol kept the fire burning!"

This time it was the Reverend who laughed loudest at his own joke.

    "Well, as I said, I'm off to see Mrs Davies."

"Well, give her our love," instructed Megan, "and tell her if she needs any help organising the funeral, to give us a shout."

"I will."

Dai waited until the Reverend had left.

"I suppose you think you're funny? Why did you have to mention those things? Why don't you just jack it in? Is it your sole purpose in life to give me gyp?"

"Well, for an ex-rugby player and miner you're still a little Babi-lol at heart, but you're my Babi-lol" she smiled, rubbing his head.

"Yes, and you're my little nest of vipers. Like an itch you can't scratch."

Two days later the Reverend and Mrs Tompkins were sitting having a coffee before the latter commenced the housework there. The phone rang and Mrs Tompkins went to take the call.

"Hello. This is the Reverend's house but I'm not the Reverend. I'm Mrs Tompkins. The Reverend's having a coffee, so who are you then that's phoning us, please?"

"Good morning. This is Councillor William Fresty. Would it be possible to speak to the Reverend, please?"

"Well, I will have to call him to the phone as he's not here at the moment as it's still me speaking, so one moment."

Mrs Tompkins went into the kitchen.

"Who was it, Mrs Tompkins?"

Mrs Tompkins rolled her eyes, trying to remember.

"There's a Mr 'Frosty' on the phone. Well, I think that's his name. But I might be wrong. It's a bit of a bad line and I think he thought I was you. So it must be a bad line, mustn't it?"

The Reverend went to the phone.

"Good morning. The Reverend Ivor Emmanuel speaking. How may I help you?"

"Good morning. I'm Councillor William Fresty from Cardiff Chambers of Commerce. I am phoning about the e-mail we received this morning from the Welsh government. I assume that I'm correct in thinking it's some sort of practical joke? It states that you are no longer going to be part or Wales or the United Kingdom and have decided to go independent. I just thought I would give you a courtesy call in case you were not aware of this. Obviously, it's false and sent by some practical joker. If you wish, I can send you a copy of the letter so you can try to figure out who is responsible."

The Reverend waited until he had finished.

"I can assure," he started softly, "that this is not a practical joke but completely serious. We do not have a sense of humour, er... I mean we *do* have a sense of humour but not about this. This is a very serious matter and what you have in your hand is an official document proving so."

Mr Fresty cleared his throat and for a couple of seconds seemed lost for words.

"You do know that you just can't decide that you no longer want to be part of Wales or the United Kingdom? It's not as easy as that. If it was, I could decide to become my own independent country whilst I'm sitting here in my office! You do understand what I'm saying, don't you?"

The Reverend could feel his blood pressure rising.

"Do you think we just sat around last week and decided to become independent, over a cup of coffee? We actually went - as it states in the letter - on a fact-finding mission to Europe and have full backing from a European Member of Parliament! So, I suggest you go to the head of your department and explain this to them. If you then wish to speak to me further, I will be quite happy to communicate with you. Good day to you!"

Before Mr Fresty could say anything else, the Reverend had replaced the receiver and returned to the kitchen.

"Who the hell does he think he is?" stormed the Reverend out loud.

"I think he was a 'Mr Frosty'," Mrs Tompkins replied, prompting a smile from the Reverend.

"I know his name," he replied and duly recited to her the conversation. Mrs Tompkins listened intently.

"So his name was not Mr 'Frosty,' then? Well, if he can't get his name right we have nothing to worry about really."

The Reverend shook his head in disbelief, wondering if it would be a lot nicer living in the type of world that Mrs Tompkins inhabited.

Mrs Tompkins commenced the housework, accompanied by her own singing.

"Right, then," announced the Reverend. "I'm going to hold a meeting tonight and tell everyone what those stupid people in the government thought of the letter. How dare they think it was a joke!"

With that he grabbed his coat and headed out of the door.

As always these days, the meeting was packed with villagers. Everyone shared the Reverend's annoyance, agreeing that if their independence was challenged now in anyway that they would fight tooth-and-nail to the last man standing. They would not, as Dai the Pub had said "roll over and die". "They don't know who they are messing with!" and duly came up with the slogan: "Mess with the best, end up like the rest!" Dai claimed he had made it up but in truth he had seen it on a tee-shirt on sale during the Falklands War.

The next day or so passed peacefully; then the Reverend's phone rang once more. Again Mrs Tompkins answered.

"Hello. This is Mrs Tompkins here but I'm at the Vicarage at the moment and not at home. So, if you're ringing for me you got the wrong number, and can you ring me at my home instead?"

"Good morning. This is Councillor Fresty. May I speak to the Reverend, please?"

"Oh, hello again. Are you sure you got your name right this time because you told me you were Mr 'Frosty' last time? Now, before I call the Reverend, are you sure you're the right person this time? You nearly confused me last time: we are not all tup, you know!"

The Reverend entered the hallway to intervene just as Mr Fresty was confirming his name.

"Good morning, Mr Frosty! How may I help you on this fine morning?"

"Well, first of all," commenced Mr Fresty, "I wish to apologise for assuming the other day that your letter was a practical joke. But you must understand that we have never received a letter like that before."

"May I therefore assume that if you have never seen anything before in your life that you would automatically assume it to be false? If so, then what about the Virgin Mary giving birth whilst still being a virgin? Or do you think that's false? If so, this phone call will end very quickly."

"I do not wish to discuss religion with you this morning. That's more for a Sunday in church!" replied Mr Fresty, abruptly.

"Oh, so you go to a *church* then, do you and not a *chapel*?"

"Excuse me, Reverend, but would it be possible please if we can get off the religion topic? That's not what I phoned you for this morning: I rang you hoping that you would be willing to attend a meeting to discuss the matter in hand? To make it easier for you, we would like you to meet us at Brynlog Council offices - if that's suitable for you?"

The Reverend moved the receiver away from his mouth and took a deep breath.

"Are you taking the mickey, boyo? You know we are not allowed near those council offices anymore. I suppose everyone thought it was funny when they heard about what happened there. Well, the jokes are on you lot as we returned as heroes: we were christened 'The Four Musketeers' - so put that in your pipe and smoke it, boyo!"

Mr Fresty's tone changed to shock.

"I'm sorry. I don't understand what you are taking about? Would you like to explain to me what you mean?"

"Either you don't know what I'm talking about or you're a very good actor. But then again all you councillors are good actors, otherwise you would never have become elected, would you? Anyway, it would be unacceptable to meet at Brynlog Council offices, so you will have to choose another venue for our meeting. And before you decide on a venue, we will not be coming to Cardiff or London for that matter!"

"Well, in that case, I think the best venue for our meeting will be at Aberglas, then."

"That's 'New Aberglas', boyo. One moment: let me just check my diary."

He placed the receiver close to his address book and flicked through the pages in mock consultation.

"Tomorrow or the next day seem OK. How is that for you?"

Mr Fresty agreed that tomorrow would be good for him and his fellow councillors: "We will be with you at 10am if that suits you." The Reverend agreed and replaced the receiver fully. He then picked the phone to contact Dai and Mrs Morgan Morgan, requesting their company at the *Dragon and Daffodil* by eleven o'clock to discuss matters.

Dai made the Three Musketeers a cup of coffee, with he and Mrs Morgan Morgan listening as the Reverend explained the proposal.

"We need to keep our cool tomorrow. Losing our tempers will not achieve anything!"
This was specifically directed at Mrs Morgan Morgan.

"I'm sure I don't know what you mean," she replied icily.

"Well, we must have a battle plan in place before we meet them tomorrow. Don't want to be unprepared, otherwise they are going to think that it really is a joke and not take us seriously. We could end up being the laughing stock of Wales and Cardiff - and we will never live it down."

"Did I ever tell you about the time I took on over 50 Americans single-handedly in my pub?" chipped in Dai.

"Once or twice," replied the other two wearily.

"Or what about the time I managed to swerve past the one-and-only 'Merv the Swerve' and the great J.P.R Williams at the same time, then?"

"You managed to swerve past Merv the Swerve *and* J.P.R Williams? I think you may be slightly exaggerating, Dai!"

"Not exaggerating: just plain lying more like."

"I'm telling you the truth! It was December 12th, 1974. The location was Cardiff, it was a cold day and there was ice on the roads and pavements."
Dai loved setting the scenes to anything that had happened in his life.

"I was walking along Castle Street in a North-South direction, and coming towards me in a South-North direction was Merv the Swerve and J.P.R. As I got about five yards from them, I slipped on a piece of ice and started to pelt towards them. But I managed to swerve past the pair of them - like a gazelle, I was."

Dai had, however, forgotten to mention that just after he passed them he fell to the ground like an elephant trying to roller-skate.

"That's a fascinating story, Dai," commented the Reverend, "but what's that got to do with the meeting in the morning?"

"Well, what I'm trying to say to you is, that if an amateur rugby player - who could have turned professional if he had got a lucky break - can beat two of the greatest Welsh players ever to grace the hallowed turf of Cardiff Arms Park, if he can beat them, then beating a couple of trumped-up councillors from Cardiff will be easy-peasy lemon squeezy. But if they do decide to fight us and declare war on us, they will be so sorry…" once again breaking into his best Winston Churchill tones, "never will two lambs be slaughtered so quickly: they will become the first casualties of war."

"I am sure that Winston Churchill never mentioned 'lambs to the slaughter'?" sighed Mrs Morgan Morgan.

"I actually think it's mentioned in the Bible but I can't do Jesus as I don't know what he sounded like. But saying that, I bet he had a Welsh accent though!" and burst out laughing.

Chapter Ten

Peace talks

The following day at 6am found Dai and Colin standing by the 'Welcome' sign to the village. Colin was clutching a new signpost whilst Dai was busy trying to remove the old one. Colin had gone to Swansea a couple of days earlier, shopping with Linda, and had found somewhere that made metal signs. He then came up with a brainwave: to order a new one for the village and collect it at the same time as he picked up the new flag: "I might not be good enough for the new police force or driving through snow but no doubt everyone will appreciate what I did!" he proclaimed with satisfaction, proudly holding the new sign in his outstretched arms.

Meanwhile, Dai was still trying to remove the last rusty bolt from it. The other three had proved slightly easier but the last one seemed to be putting up a fight.

"Do me a favour, butte. Grab the persuader out of my toolbox, will you?"

Colin went to Dai's toolbox. After a couple of seconds rummaging, he looked up at Dai.

"What's a 'persuader'? And are you sure you put one in?"

Dai walked over to him and picked up a hammer from the box.

"There you go: one persuader!"

"But that's a hammer."

"Yes, but believe me, when I use it it will 'persuade' the bolt to move!"

With that, Dai placed the spanner back on the rusty bolt and lifted the hammer to commence gently tapping away it. Unfortunately, it was to no avail. After about ten taps Dai started to lose his temper, finally lifting the hammer up high over his head before closing his eyes and slamming the hammer down hard on to the spanner.

The result was a bit of good luck for Dai – but a bit of bad luck for Colin. Dai had been standing close to the bolts when he had managed to extract the first three but had decided to stand at arms-length for the fourth to make sure he was at a safe distance from hitting himself with the hammer instead of the bolt. As the hammer hit the spanner, the spanner shot off and smashed smack into Colin's taxi's right headlight.

"Are you mental, mun? Look what you done to my beautiful car!"

"Well, technically I did not do it. It was the spanner that smashed the light, not me. Anyway, you are bound to have some collateral damage in war time! But just think though….if they try and attack us now, we now have a new weapon: the spanner and hammer!"

"I'm not the enemy, you div! I'm on our side."

Colin walked over to survey the damage to the light, shaking his head as he went.

"Sorry, butte," shouted Dai. "I think it's what they call 'friendly fire'. Do me a favour, though. Can you fetch the spanner back as I think it moved the bolt that time?"

He then had to duck as Colin picked up the spanner and threw it as hard as he could towards Dai. The spanner landed just behind him.

"Nice throw, mate but you missed the target!"

The bolt finally gave up its resistance, allowing Dai to remove the old signpost. He called Colin for assistance in erecting its replacement.

"So, are you going to pay for that?"

"Don't be tup, mun. You're insured aren't you?"

"Yes, for third party, fire and theft but not for spanner and hammer!"

"OK. I will pay half as it was partly my fault. Now let's talk about this later and get this sign up."

Ten minutes later Dai and Colin stood in front of the new sign; both smiled proudly.

"Well, anyone now who drives past the sign will know they are now entering a new country."

The sign read croeso I aberglas newydd cymru newydd os gwelwchyn dda mae eich pasbortau barod

Translated, it read: 'Welcome to New Aberglas New Wales: please have your passports ready.' They had decided to omit the part telling non-Welsh speakers "to bugger off" in case they needed some friendly allies in the event of a war. Yet if any non-Welsh speakers did start annoying them, they would be arrested, taken to the country's border and then banned for life - or even longer - from ever entering the country again.

The pair then returned in Colin's slightly blinded car to Dai's pub. By this time Colin had calmed down – especially after Dai had promised to pay for half the damage to it. As they sat in the kitchen waiting for the kettle to boil, Megan came downstairs in her nightie.

"Morning love."

Megan was still half-asleep.

"Morning Dai. You're up early, love. Hello Colin."

She then jolted awake.

"Colin, close your eyes!"

With that she whirled back upstairs. Dai laughed and put their coffees on the table. Colin just sat there with his eyes closed.

"It's all right, butte. You can open them now. She's gone upstairs."

Colin cautiously opened one eye first followed by the other. Megan returned five minutes later.

"Glad to see you're dressed this time, love. Normally she walks around naked. You were lucky she was cold last night!" and burst out laughing again.

Megan grabbed her cup from the drainer and made herself a cup of tea.

"I will have you know that the only time I'm naked is when I'm in the bath - and then the door is closed and the light is off! Me walk around naked? In your dreams, boy Bach!"

"I was only winding you up, love. Honestly, she never walks around naked: she usually has thigh-high boots on!"

"If I had thigh-high boots, Dai, they would at the moment be kicking your ass around the kitchen!"

Megan paused, remembering Colin's presence.

"Er, not that it is not nice to see you, Colin, but why are you here so early?"

Colin just sat there without saying a word, drinking his coffee.

"He just had a car accident," filled in Dai, "but it's OK: only a little bit of damage. Neither of us was hurt, thank goodness."

"Are you sure you're OK? You're looking a bit pale."

"The reason I think he looks pale, Megan, is that he just saw you nearly naked. I'm used to it - and it still shocks me!"

Colin and Dai laughed heartily at this - much to Megan's annoyance.

"Well, it will be a long time before you see me naked again, Dai, after that last remark. Anyway, what happened? How did the accident occur?"

"Let me tell this one, Colin," insisted Dai. "Well, the thing is, Colin was parked up and he was helping me put the new village sign up. Then all of a sudden a spanner shot across the road and smashed into his right-hand headlight. It was quite astonishing and a fluke."

Megan surveyed Colin.

"Was this idiot," she asked looking back at Dai, "using a hammer to hit something with?"

Colin nodded.

"You are the only man I know who would put a greenhouse up using a hammer! You're not down the mines anymore. When you're working above ground you have got to be more careful. You might kill someone someday: then you will be sorry."

"I won't be as sorry as the person I hit though!" quipped Dai, trying in vain to bring a smile to Megan's face. "You should see the new sign: it's really tidy like. Makes us proud to be 'New Aberglassens' and it will let everyone know we are a new country now. There's no mistake."

"Just a quick question," said Megan. "The new sign is at the Llancoch road end of the village or the Brynlog end?"

"The Llancoch road end."

"So, anyone coming in from the Brynlog end will not know that they are entering a new country?"

"Well, in that case let's hope everyone comes in from the Llancoch end, so they will know!"

"Why didn't you get two signs, Colin?" muttered Dai. "Did you not think of the other end?"

Dai then paused for a moment trying to formulate a solution.

"Hang on. I got an idea: if we go down and take a photo of the new sign we can get it developed and made bigger. We can then stick it on the Brynlog end, and in case it rains we can wrap it in clingfilm. Bet you never knew you married a genius, did you?" he beamed back at his wife.

"How do you know about my other husband?"

"What do you mean, love?"

"Well, for me to have married a genius I would have had to have married one: you're no member of Mensa, are you?"

"The way he used that hammer," piped up Colin, "he's more densa than Mensa!"

The Reverend looked at his watch as he entered the village hall: 9.15am. Dai had arrived at 8.45 and moved two large tables together to the centre of the room. He had also enlisted Colin to place the new flag on the wall so that when Brynlog's councillors took their seats, they would be facing it.

"Morning Dai," greeted the Reverend. "How are you today?"

"All right, Rev. All ready for the battle then, is you?

"It's not going to to be a war meeting, Dai. I told you that we need to play clever. If we go in head first we might lose the battle. We need to be cool, calm and collected: slowly, slowly, catchy monkey!"

"So you admit it's a battle, then? And anyway, we are not trying to catch a monkey, we are trying to prove that we are independent. The nearest place I know that's got monkeys is Bristol zoo - and I tell you what, you would never catch them if you were going slowly! I have seen them fly through the trees as if their asses were on fire - and judging by the colour of their bums, it looks as if they are!"

At that moment Mrs Morgan Morgan entered the room, dressed in black as always.

"Good morning to you both!"

"Good morning Mrs Morgan Morgan."

"Hi Di."

"If you are going to be an annoying prat this morning, David the Public House, I will leave now - and without me you don't stand a chance in hell of winning."

"I'm only joking....good morning Mrs Morgan Morgan. How are you this morning? Hope you slept well - and may I ask if you would like a cup of tea or coffee?"

"That's better - and thank you. Yes, I would like a cup of coffee."

"Well, at times like this I just wish we had a kettle, cups and coffee here. If we did, I would have made you one, no problem. I would go back to the *Drag and Daff* and get you one but I might miss the beginning of the meeting. And as you said, you won't win without me."

"I said, 'You won't win without *me*'," scowled Mrs Morgan Morgan.

"That's right: 'me'."

"OK, let's calm this down," ordered the Reverend. "We all need to sing from the same hymn book this morning. Now, I suggest we go through the questions and answers we wrote out, before they turn up. We need to know these off by heart. They should be here in about half an hour so let's get cracking!"

The three of them started their brain-storming. Twenty minutes later they heard two cars pull up outside the hall.

"Action stations, everyone," shouted Dai: "It's time for battle!"

They all took a deep breath, then Dai rose from his chair.

"I will go and greet them officially like, to show we aren't common like."

"I think it would be better if *I* greeted them," insisted Mrs Morgan Morgan.

"If you go they are going to think they are attending a wake, not an official meeting."

"We will all go," sighed the Reverend. "So no more arguing. We are supposed to be on the same side."

Before they had reached the door, Mr Fresty had already entered followed by two colleagues: a Mr Simpson and a Miss Williamson.

"Good morning. You must be the Reverend!" declared Mr Fresty.

"Well, there's no fooling you!" quipped Dai to him. "Is it because he has his dog collar on or was it just a lucky guess?"

"It was a lucky guess," he replied, trying to repel Dai's joke.

"OK then, for two points: which one of us is Mrs Morgan Morgan?"

"Is it you?" he grimaced, pointing at Dai.

"No, it's the one with the moustache!"

Mr Fresty paused to let the remark die before introducing his two colleagues. They then took their seats at the table.

"I would firstly like to take this opportunity," commenced Mr Fresty, "to thank you for agreeing to meet with us this morning. Miss Williamson here will be taking Minutes of the meeting, and if you require a copy of them can you please give her your e-mail addresses now? She will then e-mail the Minutes to you. I am also hoping that after this meeting we will put this silly proposal to bed, and go back to being normal again."

"Let me tell you, boyo: we will never be normal again!" Dai then realised what he said and sheepishly sat back down.

"May I take your e-mail address first?" asked Miss Williamson of Dai, "as I need to ensure I get it right."

She opened her notepad ready. Dai just stared at her.

"What's an e-mail? Is it like a third-class stamp?"

"You're so funny!" she giggled.

But Dai was serious.

"Your e-mail address. You know? Your electronic mail on your computer?"

"Oh right. Sorry. Got a bit confused then. Never heard it called that before. But do you have to have a computer for one of those mail things 'cos I don't have one, nor does the Reverend."

Miss Williamson turned her attention to Mrs Morgan Morgan.

"Can you give me your address then, please?"

"Certainly. It's Mrs Morgan Morgan, 55 Tree Line Road."

"*Mrs Morgan Morgan. 55 Tree Line Road @ ...?*" wrote Miss Williamson, and looked once again at Mrs Morgan Morgan.

"...at the end of this road: turn left and you're there. You should have said, 'Where is it?' not 'at'; that's very poor grammar, I must say."

"It's OK, interrupted Mr Fresty. "I will ensure that the Minutes of this meeting will be delivered by a courier instead. Now, would it be possible to start the meeting as we have a lot to go through this morning and I do have a formal dinner to attend in Cardiff this evening?"

"Hey, butte. How many people go to these formal dinners, then?" enquired Dai.

"Usually between 50 and 100," replied Mr Fresty, "but may I ask why you're interested?"

"Well, we do food up the *Drag and Daff.* I could sort you out a bit of a discount if you fetched 100 people with you. I would give you your dessert for half price! You scratch my back and I scratch yours too," he winked. "Remind me to give you a menu later."

Mr Fresty regarded the three people before him.

"So first of all, could you please explain the reason for wanting to go independent from Wales and indeed the United Kingdom? We have never heard of anyone wanting to do this before - or is it just a publicity stunt? I do remember the story of the self-propelled coffin some years back when your village made the television and newspapers. Is this proposal just to try to get back into the limelight?"

"Listen, you jumped-up little prat!" screamed Mrs Morgan Morgan. "This is serious. It's not some little 'publicity stunt' as you called it. We are going to go independent as we are fed up to the back teeth with you lot trying to rule us with an iron fist. You're like that stupid little man in Russia years ago."

"She means 'Stanley'," volunteered Dai.

Mr Fresty looked confused.

"Excuse me. Who's Stanley?"

"The little man in Russia she's talking about. His name was 'Stanley'."

"You mean 'Stalin'?" suggested the Reverend.

"That's it," lied Dai. "Stanley Stalin."

Mrs Morgan Morgan let Dai stew.

"The main reason," she continued, "for us to go independent is that you tried to make us twin with a village somewhere in Outer Mongolia. You thought we would just roll over and accept it. Well, this time you got it wrong. You never asked us if we wanted to go from pound notes to pound coins years ago either! Well, you have a fight on your hands this time, I'm telling you straight."

"So you're telling me that the only reason you want to go independent is because you don't want to twin with a village? It seems a massive fuss over something so small. You only had to make an appointment and then we could have talked this over before it reached this stage of proceedings."

"Are you trying to wind us up? You must have heard of the commotion that happened after we went to Brynlog to speak to the Mayor and ended up being escorted out of the building by a couple of trumped-up traffic wardens? We went there in peace and ended up being frog-marched out like tresspassers and banned from ever going again!"

"Oh, that was you, was it? I'm sorry I did not know. I have heard the story but you know what it's like: by the time the story gets to the last person things have been either added or taken away. 'Chinese whispers' I think they call it?"

"Well, at least you're not going to be the last person to find out this time. You are going to be the first one," announced Dai, "and also you are the first outsiders to enter our new country, too. So congratulations. But I must ask you though, did you fetch your passports with you? You should really show them when you crossed the border but as you are delegates of old Wales we will let you off this time. But if you ever want to come back, please ensure you bring your passports with you. Otherwise you may be refused entry - unless you claim political asylum, and in that case we might allow you to stay for a couple of weeks until it's safe to go back to your own country. But if you are going to claim asylum, can you ring us first in case we are fully booked? I would try to avoid July and August as it's the busiest time of the year. I remember once I could not get in to any Bed & Breakfast in Tenby as it was the summer holidays."

"Dai," interrupted the Reverend, "I think we should leave your holiday tales for a later date and get back to the matters in hand. As Mrs Morgan Morgan said, the main reason for us going independent is that we are fed up with being told what is going to happen to us without asking our opinion first. For this reason we have decided to go independent: we will make our own decisions from now on and not be dictated to anymore - and we have the full backing of everyone who lives here."

"So," summarised Mr Fresty, "the only reason we are here today is because you don't want to be twinned with another European village? It seems you're making a mountain out of a molehill and to be perfectly honest with you, I think you're not only wasting your time but ours also!"

"Well in that case I think you should leave as you're no longer welcome in our country. And if you don't leave peacefully we will be forced to extradite you. And when you get back to Brynlog please inform them that despite the peace talks breaking down, we are still a peaceful country and will still be going forward with our independence."

Mr Fresty reeled at this outburst from Mrs Morgan Morgan.

"Are you trying to tell my colleagues and I that we are being extradited from here? This is not some political coup, for goodness sake! I only live 22 miles away and I can assure you that I will come and go in this little village of yours whenever I please! You cannot do anything about it. All I can assume is that you have spent too long between the mountains that surround this place and have been starved of oxygen so giving you this illusion of grandeur! When you finally wake up and smell the coffee, you will understand that this is just a stupid idea. If *Beadle's About* was still on television I would have expected him to come into the room with a cameraman now, saying this has all been a hoax!"

"I will be back in five minutes," announced Dai. "But if I'm not back in five minutes, wait longer!"

An awkward silence ensued, eventually to be broken by the Reverend.

"I would just like to thank you for coming over to us this morning but unfortunately it seems to be a stalemate. However, as Mrs Morgan Morgan said, we will still be going ahead with our independence from the rest of Wales and the United Kingdom."

"So I'm assuming this meeting is finished and that there is no resolution? Well, before I go I will inform you that we are opposed to your idea and will use every available force to quash this farce!"

With that he gestured to his colleagues to head for the door. As they did so they were met by Dai and P.C. Williams.

"Sit back down, butte boy. You ain't going anywhere!"

"What do you mean, 'We are not going anywhere?' As I explained to the other two, you don't have a snowball's chance in Hell of going independent."

"Why does everything that's said to me have to involve the word 'Hell'? I know I'm going there so stop going on about it!"

"What do you mean, you're going to Hell?" blasted Mr Fresty at him, with incredulity. "You're already there - and I'm positive that's the Devil's daughter sitting there and I assume…" he said, pointing at the Reverend, "instead of going up to Heaven he went down to Hell by mistake?"

"How dare you! Don't you dare talk about my friends like that! You have no right. You don't know how much they are liked in this village. If I had the money I would erect a statue of the both of them. Now: apologise!"

Dai was genuinely livid while Mrs Morgan Morgan's sat in shock at the way Dai had just stood up to them on her behalf.

"I apologise," muttered Mr Fresty. "I did not mean any harm."

"That's better," said Dai. "Now please retake your seats. I think I have a resolution that will benefit both parties."

They sat back down, with Dai and P.C. Williams standing beside them. Dai pulled out two pieces of paper from his coat pocket.

"Here you go."

Mr Fresty took the papers from Dai and started to read them. He kept looking up at the publican and then back to the pages before putting them down on the table.

"Do you really think that I'm going to sign these? If so, you're very much mistaken. Let me tell you, it will be a cold day in Hell before I do!"

"See? The word 'Hell' again? Well, if it's going to be a cold day in Hell I think I had better be buried with shorts and a jumper on, for when it's hot and cold then!" quipped Dai to him, smiling. Dai took the papers from the table.

"So, are you going to sign these or not?"

"For the first and last time: I am not going to sign these stupid pieces of paper - and if you think that this so-called police officer is going to make me do it, you are very much mistaken. Let me tell you, in my life I have dealt with bigger and better than you lot, so don't think you scare me!"

"He's not here to threaten you, he is here to witness the documents as a representative of the law - you know, to make it all official like."

"Well, unfortunately you have wasted your time coming here. Have you thought about going out and catching some real criminals like you're supposed to?"

"Are you refusing to sign this document, sir?" enquired P.C. Williams.

"I am not going to sign it."

"Well, in that case, may I see your passport please?"

"What the hell are you on about, man? I don't carry it around with me. I only have it when I'm going abroad!"

"Then," pondered Dai, surveying Mr Fresty's companions, "Do either of you have your passports with you?" They both looked at each other and then shook theirs heads.

"Well, in that case," sighed P.C. Williams, "I am detaining the three of you on suspicion of entering this country illegally! Anything you say can - and most definitely will - be used against you!"

"Don't be so stupid, man! You can't detain us under some stupid law you made up. Now get out of my way before you have to arrest me for punching a pretend policeman who should have retired, by the looks of things, a long time ago."

"Well, in that case sir, I am now going to arrest you instead for threatening a police officer - and I have five witnesses to prove it."

"Did you hear me threaten this man?" he asked of his two colleagues. But before they could answer, Dai spoke up.

"Remember, he said, anything you say is going to go against you in a court of law. I always wanted to say that!"

"Well," Miss Williamson said to Mr Fresty, "you did actually say you were going to punch him, so it was sort of a threat."

"I rest my case," beamed Dai. "Truth. You can't handle the truth. I loves that film *A Few Dollars More,* whispered Dai, turning to the Reverend.

"Actually the film is, *A Few Good Men',"* corrected Miss Williamson.

"Yes, but I bet after the amount of money they made on the film, the actors got 'a few dollars more' in their wage packet!"

Once more Dai tried to bury his own error.

"This is ridiculous! I'm going to phone the real police." Mr Fresty retrieved his mobile phone from his inside pocket and went to press the keypad.

"Damn! There's no signal in here. One moment."

Unfortunately for him, Dai was blocking his exit.

"Oh, butte. You only get one phone call: book him Dano!" Dai roared out laughing.

"I'm sorry, sir," intervened P.C. Williams, "but I can't allow you to go outside as you're under arrest."

"Please ring Brynlog police, Miss Williamson, and tell them that I'm being held against my will!"

"Er, I have no signal!"

Mr Fresty looked at his other companion.

"Do *you* have a signal?"

"No, sorry I don't either."

"Well, it must be the mountains," surmised the Reverend. "The trouble is, as you said earlier, that we are starved of oxygen and mobile phone signals here. Does your mobile phone have a signal, Dai?"

"I'm not sure. I will have to go and buy one to check if it does. Where's the nearest phone shop?"

"Brynlog, I think."

"You going back that way, Mr Fresty? If so, can I have a lift, please? Oh, sorry. I forgot you're under arrest. Never mind! I will get one tomorrow."

P.C. Williams confronted Mr Fresty.

"Now sir: are you going to come quietly or do I have to put handcuffs on you?"

"Slap the bracelets on him!" squealed Dai. "I think that's from *The Godfather* or something."

"This is ridiculous! By the time I finish with you, you won't be able to help an old lady across the road or even tell someone the time."

"That's no problem," retorted P.C Williams. "Everyone has got a watch in Aberglas, so they never ask me."

"This can all go away if you just sign these two declarations of independence," declared the Reverend calmly. "Why don't you just sign them, boyo? It's only a signature and I am sure P.C. Williams will forget the charge of threatening behaviour as well."

"If you don't sign it," boomed Miss Williamson, "I will! I just want to go home."

With that she sat down and started crying.

"Now look what you done!" snapped Dai. "She is so upset I don't think she will ever want to come here on holiday now - and we are going to rely on the tourist trade."

Mr Fresty looked at Miss Williamson and then at Dai. Taking a very deep breath, he conceded.

"Give me a pen, man, for goodness sake!"

Mr Fresty signed his name in temper at the bottom of the documents.

"There! You happy now?"

He slammed Dai's pen onto the table with such force that the pen snapped in half. Dai retrieved the pieces.

"Well, thanks for that. I passed you an Aberglas pen and now I got a Welsh pen."

"What you talking about, a 'Welsh pen'?"

"It's a Welsh pen now, butte. See…pen broke…like as in 'pen-brook docks'."

"That's 'Pem'-broke not 'pen'-broke!"

"It's not a 'pem'; it's a 'pen'. You're such a div, you know that?"

"Thank you Mr Fresty for your time," intervened the Reverend. "May I wish you a safe and pleasant journey home."

Mr Fresty looked at him in disgust.

"Oh, and one other thing before I go: about the fire engine…no, you can't borrow one off us! You have not heard the last of this either, I assure you!"

With that Mr Fresty stormed outside followed by his colleagues. A few minutes later he returned.

"Is this a joke?" he demanded.

"No. If you had knocked the door twice, however, I would have said 'Who's there?' Now, that's a joke!"

"What seems to be the problem?" enquired the Reverend, realising that he was no longer referring to a specific agenda matter.

"Some idiots have parked their cars and blocked me in. I can't go forward or backwards."

"Well, you will have to get a lift with your friends, then."

"They have already left, heading back to Cardiff. They were on the opposite side of the road and I told them I did not need their help, so they have gone."

"Let's go and see if we can resolve this problem," suggested Mrs Morgan Morgan, and the five of them went outside.

The car parked behind Mr Fresty's vehicle was Dai's; in front of him was Colin the Cabbie's.

"Well, do you know who these cars belong to?" fumed Mr Fresty.

"Well, that one," mused Dai pointing to the car parked behind Mr Fresty's, "is mine, and the other one is Colin the Cabbie's."

"Well then, can you move your car so I can leave this Godforsaken place?"

"Well normally, butte, I would. But I had a bit of a cold this morning and I took some medicine and it says on the bottle it might cause drowsiness and not to drive heavy machinery. So I better not: don't want an accident, do I?"

"It's not heavy machinery though, is it?"

"Well, actually it is. First of all it's a driving machine - and you try lifting it up: it's really heavy. So that makes it 'heavy machinery'!"

Colin the Cabbie then approached.

"Is this your car?"

"Sorry? What did you say?"

Mr Fresty repeated his question but more slowly this time:

"Is. This. Your. Car?"

"I'm sorry," replied Colin, imitating Mr Fresty's slower tones. "I'm sorry, I don't speak your language. Do you speak Aberglassen by any chance as I no spekie your language?"

Mr Fresty looked fit to burst.

"Will you tell him to move that heap of junk?" he barked at the Reverend.

Dai shook his head.

"We got a bit of a problem there. Sorry, butte. He only speaks Aberglassen and none of us has learnt the language yet."

Mr Fresty finally snapped and threw his car keys at Colin. Colin ducked out of the way so that Mr Fresty's keys instead bounced off the kerb and fell into a drain.

"Now look what you made me do!" Where's the nearest phone? I am going to have to get a taxi home now as my spare set is in my house."

"You want a taxi, mate? Where do you want to go? This is my taxi right here. Hop in."

"I would not get in that piece of junk if it was the last car on earth! Now, where's the nearest public phone box?"

"The nearest one is about 50 yards down the road but if you want a lift home by taxi, you're going to have to meet them at the border as they won't have a valid new Aberglassen taxi certificate. Do you want a taxi to the border, butte? It will only cost you about 3 Glas."

Mr Fresty turned his back on Colin and faced the other four.

"You have not heard the last of this!"

The four of them watched Mr Fresty marching down the road. He was in such a temper he was nearly running.

"Well, that went well. Thought he would have put up a bit of an argument but he seemed quite happy to sign the documents."

"It's a good job he did," agreed P.C Williams. "Really, I was a bit worried for a moment."

"You had the law on your side," responded the Reverend, "and when he threatened you with violence you had every right to arrest him."

"I know that, Reverend. I have actually been a policeman for quite a while. That was not my concern. I was worried because the thing is, that I have lost the key to my cells. I think someone has stolen it."

"You left them in the pub last night," shrieked Dai, laughing. "I think they must have fallen out of your pocket when you were having a drink – off-duty, of course."

"I'm never off duty unless I'm in the pub!" At this he burst out laughing himself.

A couple of days later the phone rang in the pub.

"Hello, the *Dragon and Daffodil.* Dai speaking. How may I help you?"

"Hello Dai! It's Dai the Inn here. How's you, mun? Life good, is it?"

"Hello Dai. Life's tidy. What's up? You phoning to tell me Megan's banned from your place for fighting?"

"Would you try and ban your Megan?" laughed Dai the Inn. "I know sometimes I get fed up but I have never been suicidal. Anyway, the reason I'm phoning you is to give you a warning: last night I overheard a conversation between one of the councillors from across the road and another one I didn't recognise. They had had quite a few to drink and one of them was getting really angry."

"What's he look like?"

"Quite tall if you was a midget, and with greyish black hair."

"That's Mr Fresty. Good friend of mine he is."

"Well, I think he's gone off you as I overheard him telling the other one that he was going to sort out that place once and for all - and especially that div of a barman! So I knew he was talking about you."

"You cheeky bugger! I'm not a barman anyway."

"He said," continued Dai the Inn ignoring his correction, "that they were going to come back over your place tomorrow with a solicitor and the police and are going to come in the Llancoch end to get you unawares. So I thought I would give you the heads up, like."

"That's good to know. Cheers butte for that, and as you did me a favour I will do you one. If you ever fancy a nice short break I will give you mates rates at the *Drag and Daff* and I won't charge you full price. But you will have to sleep on the sofa - but I will chuck in a breakfast for free."

Dai the Inn was silent for a moment.

"Do wish you had told me that earlier. I just booked a week's holiday in Snowdonia Park for a fortnight. Maybe next year? Take care, butte. Speak soon."

Dai the Pub immediately phoned the Reverend and Mrs Morgan Morgan.

"Emergency meeting: *Drag and Daff* now. The kettle's on."

After Dai had lengthily finished explaining to the other two Mr Fresty's intentions, they decided to mount a human road block on the Llancoch side in the morning.

"United we stand, divided we fall!" proclaimed the Reverend, explaining that it was also perfectly legal to form a human roadblock as a result of the declaration that had been signed - even if it was not legal in the eyes of the law. They then all had another coffee.

"Just to let you know, I have designed some new safety posters," announced the Reverend, "which Mrs Griffiths is going to draw more professionally, about the danger of fires given that they won't lend us a fire engine."

"No need to worry about a fire engine, Rev. Forgot to tell you: one of the lads I used to play rugby with popped over yesterday for a pint and I was telling him what was going on. I actually mentioned the lack of a fire engine and luckily for us his nephew runs a travel agent's who deal with a lot of stag and hen weekends. Well, one of the vehicles he uses is an old fire engine, and he said we can borrow it when it's not booked out. The only thing is though, it has his logo and phone number on the doors and sides, so I promised him that if we had a fire and were racing to it, that if we passed a crowd of people we would slow down so they could see the advert."

P.C. Williams then walked in.

"Glad you're still here. Got some interesting news for you. I just had a phone call off one of my friends from Cardiff police and he says that him and John, my other friend, have been told they are to head over here tomorrow with that Fresty man. It's so funny that the two policemen to be assigned actually play on the same snooker team as me: it must be a sign from up above!"

"That's what we were just discussing," smiled the Reverend, "but when you see the pair of them next, thank them for telling us as I'm sure they could have got into trouble for doing so."

"They were happy to help. They have never liked Fresty since he put his idea of bobbies on the beat into action. It now means that instead of driving around they have to walk everywhere, whatever the weather. So to say he is Mr Popular with the guys at the station is a bit far from the truth."

"Any idea what time they coming over as we need to be there to stop them?" enquired Dai.

"Not sure. Sorry. The lads said it's in the morning sometime so it could be anytime between seven and midday. They could not be more precise than that."

"In that case," clapped the Reverend, "we will all meet at 6.30 in the morning and I completely understand if you don't want to be part of it, P.C. Williams, as it would not look good if you were part of the protests."

"Oh, I will be there but in my official capacity and don't worry, we got it all worked out. Well, I must be on my way now. I got a locksmith coming over in an hour to put new locks on my cellar as I have lost that damn set again."

"What does he mean, 'It's sorted in an official capacity'?" Mrs Morgan Morgan asked.

"No idea," replied the Reverend.

"If he says it's covered, it will be," reassured Dai. "Don't worry! We got the law on our side: what can go wrong?"

The Reverend was about to put his cup of coffee to his lips, when he had a thought.

"This road block, tomorrow. Would it not be easier just to put two cars across the road instead of a human road block?"

"It's more of a stand if we do it," maintained Dai. "I remember watching some man stand in front of a tank years ago on the television and it made worldwide news."

"Did the tank stop or go over him because that's a bit of a stupid thing to do! I think that's just asking for trouble," asserted Mrs Morgan Morgan.

"It stopped! If not, he would have ended up in a hospital in beds three and four."

"How do you mean, 'beds three *and* four'?"

"Because he would have been as flat as a pancake. He would have ended up being about 10-foot tall and 20-foot wide. It would have squashed him! Now do you get it?"

"Yes but I don't think it's funny. Let me tell you, if they come tomorrow morning in a tank I for one will not be standing in its way. I'm putting my foot down with a firm hand on that one, I can assure you!"

"I really don't think that Mr Fresty will be in a tank with a solicitor and two policemen," laughed the Reverend. "I think they will most probably turn up in a car."

"Well, I'm not going to stand in front of a car, either! What would happen if he did not stop or his brakes failed, and hit me over?"

"Well, the car would be a write-off for a start Mrs Morgan Morgan!"

"Well, I'm glad to see you're back to your old self. You had me worried before with what you said at the meeting."

"What do you mean? What did I say?"

"Well, when that Mr Fresty was rude to the Reverend and myself, you said he had no right to do so and defended our honour somewhat."

Dai slowly recalled the moment.

"Don't get too excited about that, love. The only reason I had a go at him is because first of all, he does not know either of you, and secondly he had no right to say it, and thirdly it's my job to take the micky out of the pair of you - not anyone else's! And you know when I take the micky out of you, I'm only serious!"

"Dai, I really think that deep down you actually have a soft spot for Mrs Morgan Morgan, really."

"Damn! You found out. OK, it's time to come clean once and for all."

Dai then turned to Mrs Morgan Morgan and rested his hand on top of hers.

"I must admit, in front of the Reverend, that I do honestly have a very soft spot for you: it's a swamp at the bottom of the beer garden!"

Mrs Morgan Morgan snatched her hand away and with one quick movement slapped it back down hard on the back of Dai's hand. Dai yelped.

"Why did you do that? I just declared my undying love for you and now you're hitting me!"

"Well, you know what they say, David the Public House? Love hurts!"

It was Mrs Morgan Morgan's turn to laugh, happy that not only had she got one over on him but that she had also inflicted pain.

"When you two have stopped flirting with each other we need to discuss the plan for tomorrow morning. Who are we going to get to help us become a human road block? I am right in assuming that the three of us will be there?"

"That's without a doubt, and I think I can persuade Colin the Cabbie to join us, as long as he doesn't put his meter on, that is."

"Is Colin the Cabbie related to you, by any chance?" enquired Mrs Morgan Morgan.

"I don't think so but I can check. What makes you think that we might be related, though?"

"Well, you are both tight buggers. You two are so tight, neither of you would even give a door a slam!"

"Oh! I'm cut to the quick. My quick has never been cut so quickly, I can tell you!"

"What did you just say, Dai? Can you repeat it slower, please?"

"You must be joking if you think I'm going to try and repeat that! I nearly fainted saying it the first time."

"Right then. Back to the plan," resumed the Reverend. "There's the three of us and hopefully Colin the Cabbie but we could really do with another."

"How about Mrs Griffiths', the school teacher's husband Mr Griffiths? After all he is now P.C. Williams' second-in-command, so at least we would have two police officers on the front line with us," suggested Mrs Morgan Morgan.

"Well, Colin usually comes in tonight for a quick pint before going home, so I will ask him then. Don't worry though, he will agree, no problem. I'm sure of that."

"How can you be so sure?" asked the Reverend.

"Well, if he doesn't, when he applies for a new hackney carriage licence from the new Aberglassen government or, to put it another way, the three of us, he could be declined. And without that he will not be able to operate as a cabbie! So. I think that's sorted, don't you?"

"So, we are the New Aberglas government, are we? When was that decided? I don't remember a vote," protested Mrs Morgan Morgan.

"Going on well. It's obvious, isn't it? We are the three pioneers of this independency. We were automatically made the government, with the three of us in joint charge. The Reverend is in charge of all matters concerning health and spiritual well-being and myself is in charge of leisure and recreation. And you, Mrs Morgan Morgan, you are in charge of medical and military matters."

"What do you mean, I am in charge of that? I understand the medical part but what do you mean, 'military matters'? I don't have any experience in that."

"Well, they go hand-in-hand really. If anyone tries to invade we will put you on the front line. You would scare anyone away! And if they were stupid enough to try and fight you, I can honestly say they would end up either in hospital or dead."

This time Dai was quick enough to dodge her hand.

"I think you might have to come up with a better tactic than that, Mrs Morgan Morgan: Dai saw that one coming!"

"Anyway, I will pop in and see Mr Griffiths on my way back home and try to persuade him to join us. Now, better get on. Got an emergency delivery due soon, and knowing Megan she will have not moved the empty barrels outside ready. The trouble is that women only want equal rights when it does not involve anything dirty or heavy!"

Mrs Morgan Morgan turned around at this.

"I have to ask, was your mother a weight-lifter when she was younger?"

"Don't be daft, mun. She was a gentle and kind wife and mother. What makes you ask that?"

"Well, it's because she must have been to have raised a dumb-bell like you!"

With that, she marched triumphantly out of the door.

Chapter Ten

Live and Let Dai

The rain hit Dai's bedroom window so hard it woke him. He looked at his digital clock: 05.55.

"I still should have five minutes before the alarm goes off," he groaned.

Megan was fast asleep, gently snoring loudly. Dai had often told her that she snored but she refused to believe him: "I have never heard myself snoring," she would tell him. "If I snored that badly it would wake me up, wouldn't it?"

Dai switched off the alarm before it rang and woke Megan. He put on his dressing gown and went downstairs to start the kettle and switch on the radio for the local news, followed by the weather.

The forecaster announced that there was a 75% chance of rain for Wales today. Dai looked out of the window: "I guess more like 100%", and made himself a coffee. He then smiled, remembering how Colin the Cabbie had been conned last night into joining the human road block this morning. Dai had mentioned to him the new hackney carriage licence Colin would need to be able to operate his cab in New Aberglas. But what had sealed the deal was that his once-a-month rendezvous with Wilf in Brynlog would be kept a secret. Even better, Colin would now have a perfect excuse as Dai would tell Colin's wife that he was on official New Aberglas business, taking important documents to Brynlog on behalf of the Aberglas government.

The radio broadcaster announced that it was just gone 6.20 so Dai made his way upstairs to get dressed. He switched on the lamp by his side of the bed so that he would not wake Megan but as soon as the light came on, Megan awoke.

"Dai, what you doing? It's the middle of the night, mun! You know I'm a light sleeper. Why did you not get dressed in the dark?"

"You're a light sleeper? Don't make me laugh! When you close your eyes and start snoring, a bomb could go off at the bottom of the bed and you would sleep through it! Anyway, how can I get dressed in the dark? I wouldn't know what I was putting on, would I? What happened if I put your dress on by mistake? I would be called a woolly woofter - or worse: a translucent."

"It's not a 'translucent'," groaned Megan, "it's a 'transparent', you div! Now, hurry up. Get dressed and shut the light off. I'm trying to have a lie-in: my alarm's not due to go off 'til eight!"
With that she turned over and immediately started snoring.

After Dai finished dressing, he crept over to Megan's alarm clock, turned it to 'Off' and then put the time on by an hour. He then returned to his own clock, also put it forward one hour and then set the alarm for 8am – or 7am, as it would actually be. He shut the light off and went downstairs, smugly congratulating himself upon getting his own back for her foul mood. However, thinking that the last place he wanted to be was in Megan's firing line when she realised he had changed the alarm, Dai grabbed his coat and shot out of the door.

The rain was pelting down and the cold wind hit his face. It reminded him of when he worked down the mine: he would have to walk ten miles to the pit as he could not afford a car in those days. It's funny how little things like that reminded him of the 'good old days', he thought to himself.

When Dai reached the proposed human road-block location, he found Colin and P.C. Williams already waiting in Colin's cab, drinking cups of coffee.

"Good morning, Dai. Raining out there, is it?"

"I'm not sure. Call the dog in and see if he's wet!" retorted Dai to Colin. "Now, enough of sitting in there, mun. They could turn up any minute! We need to be ready."

Mrs Morgan Morgan's car pulled up at that moment, accompanied by the Reverend and Mr Griffiths.

"Morning, Dai," greeted the Reverend. "It might be a miserable morning but I'm sure in a couple of moments you're going to have a big smile on your face! Trust me."

Mrs Morgan Morgan opened her door. As always she was wearing her black hat, long black coat and wielded her umbrella. But then Dai realised what the Reverend had actually meant, for on her feet were pink Wellington boots decorated with yellow flowers. She tried to keep her dignity as he burst into a raucous laughter so loud it could have woken Megan and half the village.

"Nice boots, Mrs Morgan Morgan. Did you put them on to make sure that the tank sees you?" he continued, almost weeping.

Mrs Morgan Morgan poked him in the stomach with her umbrella.

"Do not start annoying me at this time of the morning. Otherwise I will go home right now. These were given to me by my niece a few years back, as a joke. I normally wear my black ones but a certain cat decided to drop a dead bird in one of them, so they had to be thrown out."

"Well I'm sure that during your time when you were nursing you must have come across a deceased person? I didn't think you would be squeamish about a little dead bird!"

"I will have you know, David the Public House, that in my many years of nursing I did have to deal with a lot of deaths, unfortunately. But I cannot remember any one of them that was chewed to death by a cat, so now you know!"

"Well let's hope it's not too long before they get here," breezed the Reverend. "I don't fancy standing out here all morning in this filthy weather."

"I have an idea," announced Colin, still sitting in his cab. "Why don't we take it in turns to sit in the car for twenty minutes to dry off?"

"That's a really good idea, Colin, and very thoughtful of you." Turning to Dai, the Reverend said, "You have been here the longest, so you can go first."

"No, I don't mean my car," shouted Colin, "I mean Mrs Morgan Morgan's. I don't want my seats to get wet! This car is my livelihood. I can't expect my passengers to sit on damp seats, can I?"

"So, what happens if it's raining when you pick them up then?" enquired Mr Griffiths, speaking for the first time since arriving.

"Well, divo, I normally pick them up from their house, not the middle of a road in the middle of a tropical thunderstorm!"

"This is not a tropical thunderstorm," argued Dai. "It's a typical New Wales' summer's day, full of liquid sunshine. Now, come on, let's not argue: 'We are a team. What are we?'" to which nobody responded. So Dai tried again: 'We are a team. What are we?'"

"Wet," responded Mrs Morgan Morgan. "Now just stand here and shut up 'til you're spoken to."

The Reverend checked his watch.

"It's already a quarter to eight! Do these people know that we are getting soaked standing here? If they had any compassion, they would have turned up by now."

"The trouble is, that they don't actually know that we are standing here waiting. The thing about a surprise is that it's a surprise. If they knew we were here then the surprise would not be a surprise. I'm surprised you did not know that!" Dai suddenly thought to himself, 'Oh my God, I'm beginning to sound like Megan, and a shudder passed through him.

"I just had a thought," announced Colin the Cabbie.

"In that case, do you want to lay down for a bit? That must of hurt you!"

"No. Serious. What happens if they decide to come in the Brynlog end? There's no-one protecting that end."

A voice boomed from underneath her umbrella.

"P.C. Williams reliably informed us that they would be coming into the village from this end, and I don't think a policeman would lie to us - if he knows what's good for him that is!"

Suddenly, in the distance a car could be heard.

"Stand by, everyone! Here we go then!"

Without any practice they all walked forward and formed a straight line as the car came around the corner.

"Don't let them take the line! Fight 'til you die!"

The car then came fully into view. It was Mair and Daffydd Shop. They made it to within ten yards of the line before getting out.

"What's the matter? Why are you here to meet us? Is the shop OK?"

Before they had a chance to answer she turned to Daffydd:

"See? I told you something would happen when we were not here. It's all your fault wanting to have a romantic night away in Swansea. We should have stayed at home but, oh no, you said it will be fine. What could go wrong, you said? I knew something would: it's all your fault!"

"Mair, calm down," ordered the Reverend. "It's nothing to do with the shop. We are here waiting for the Brynlog contingent. They are going to try and sneak in here, that's all."

Mair's relief was immediately evident while Dafydd had stomped back to the car and was now sitting there with his arms folded. Mair contritely re-entered their vehicle and went to rub the rain off Daffydd's face, but he turned away from her - so Mair switched the engine back on and drove away. Dai watched them pass, with Daffydd's face still averted.

"How can anyone be so childish?" exclaimed Dai. "A grown man having a monk [mood] on. That is so childish! You would never catch me like that. Megan knows I'm the boss of our house!"

As he said this, Colin looked behind Dai.

"Hello Megan!" Colin said.

Dai spun, sheer panic etched on his face. Colin laughed as Dai realised Megan was not there after all.

"Boss of your house, are you mun? I don't think so! Perhaps when Megan's not there you are. Otherwise, just admit it: she's the boss, as in every marriage the women are."

It was another twenty minutes before a second vehicle approached them.

"Let's hope it's them this time," prayed the Reverend. "Action stations everyone!"

This time it *was* the Brynlog contingent. Mr Fresty got out, followed by the solicitor and the two police officers. He walked up to the Reverend, clutching his umbrella.

"I don't know what you're thinking, standing here. Your'e not going to stop us. We have the law of this land on our side, so please step aside."

"And a good morning to you too," replied the Reverend. "May I ask what you're hoping to achieve by coming here today, boyo?"

Mr Fresty opened his coat slightly and pulled out a brown manila envelope containing the paper he had signed at their previous encounter.

"This is my copy that you gave me. Well! This is what I think of it!"

With that he ripped it in two and rolled it into a ball.

"That's OK. I still have the other one you signed, safe and sound at home."

Mr Fresty looked desperately at the solicitor and the policemen.

"They made me sign that one under duresse!"

"You're lying. You were not in 'a dress'. What are you? Some kind of 'transparent'?"

Mr Fresty stared at Dai, and then back at the Reverend before returning his attention to Dai.

"What the hell are you talking about, man? What do you mean: I'm 'a transparent'?"

"See? He admits it now!" laughed Dai.

Mr Fresty stood there in bewilderment, trying desperately not to become too deflected.

"We are here today to demand the release of the document that you made me sign under…under…pressure. If you refuse, you will be arrested by these two real policemen - not that trumped-up traffic warden you have here!"

"And why is this little man with you?" demanded Mrs Morgan Morgan, pointing to his other companion. "Is he your bodyguard?"

"This is Mr Gordon. A solicitor. He has with him a document from the Welsh government which states officially the refusal to allow you to become independent from the rest of Wales and the United Kingdom. So, if you could go and get the document I was forced to sign, and accept the new document in Mr Gordon's possession, then this silly matter can be put to rest forever."

"Let me tell you, for the umpteenth time," proclaimed Mrs Morgan Morgan, "this is not some sort of silly idea to give you lot something to do. This is a real matter in which we have declared our independence! Can't you get that into your thick head? Or do you need it knocked into that thick skull of yours? If so, I would be pleased to oblige!"

"Did you hear that?" shouted Mr Fresty towards the two policemen. "She threatened me! You can arrest her for that!"

"That was not a threat. I was just offering to help you understand, that's all. If I threatened you, little boy, you would know about it for at least five seconds and then when you woke up afterwards - with a headache - hopefully it would have sunk in by then. That's all I'm saying to you."

Mr Fresty was now becoming really annoyed.

"Look! Get out of the way and let us pass - and before you say anything, I have this…"
Mr Fresty then put his hand inside his coat and pulled out his passport.

"Ha! Ha! Ha! Now what are you going to do?"

"That's fair enough," acknowledged Dai and moved aside.

Mr Fresty recommenced his line-breaking attempt but Dai again quickly stepped in front of him.

"Just one question, butte. You come here on an official visit, I assume? This means, at the moment, that you're actually working? Is that correct?"

"What are you talking about? Of course I am on official business! I would not come to this place otherwise."

"Well, in that case can I see your work visa please?"
"My what?!"
"I will say it slower: can I see your work visa, please?"
"I don't have one of those! You know that!" screamed Mr Fresty.

"Well, in that case, I'm sorry but you are not allowed to enter here to work unless you have one. But if you would like to apply for one and your application proves successful, you should hear from us within 28 days. Thanks for stopping by though."

Mr Fresty's rage could no longer be contained. Turning to the two policemen he demanded safe passage, "so I can pin the document Mr Gordon has in his briefcase to that little hut they call their government building."

The two policemen moved forward, only to be confronted by P.C. Williams.

"Excuse me, gentlemen. I think you will find that you're out of your boundary. I am the police officer of New Wales and I don't recall asking for your help or assistance. I believe that if you want to enter here you will have to get clearance from Interpol first."

The two policemen nodded and once out of Mr Fresty's view, one of them winked at P.C. Williams.

"What the hell are you doing?" screamed Mr Fresty to them.

"I'm sorry.He's right!" replied one of the officers. "Unless he calls for our assistance or we get clearance from Interpol we can't enter their country. He knows his stuff, you know!"

"This is an absolute farce!"

"I agree," replied Dai. "So why don't you get back inside your car, turn around and bugger off? I'm getting wet here and want to go home for a coffee. And don't try and sneak in when we are not looking, as we have just proven to you that if you do, you will be charged with entering a country illegally - and we will have a warrant issued for your arrest!"

"Pass me that document now, please Mr Gordon."
The solicitor retrieved it from his briefcase.

"Here. Take this!"

"It's OK, boyo," replied the Reverend. "Don't want it, to be honest with you. If I accept it, it will be classed as a summons which means I have to accept what is written on it."

"I will take it, mate," offered Colin the Cabbie.

"At last!" sighed Mr Fresty. "Someone normal."

"But before I take it, though, I got to ask: is it written in Aberglassen, 'cos I can't read any other language?"

"That's it! I have had enough of this. I'm leaving!"

"So, you're not going to come in for a cuppa then, are you?" smiled the Reverend. "Oh, that's right. If you do, you will end up in handcuffs and it's very difficult to drink a cuppa and hold a biscuit whilst wearing those. Never mind, maybe next time. But remember: you're always welcome."

Mr Fresty sped off, with Dai and the others waving them on their way.

"Well, that was easy. Now, I'm going home to have a nice hot shower. I'm soaked to the bones… and I suggest you all do the same."

Dai then noticed that Mrs Morgan Morgan had her eyes closed and was swaying slightly.

"Are you all right? Your'e looking a bit peaky."

"Of course I'm OK," she retorted, opening her eyes fully. "There's nothing wrong with me. Now let's get off home. This is not my idea of fun standing in the rain."

"Any chance of a lift to the *Drag and Daff?*" Dai asked Colin. "Don't fancy walking back."

"Sure. Hop in."

Colin pulled up outside Dai's pub.

"There we go, butte. That's 2 Glas, mate!"

"Sorry, mate. Got no Glas on me. Only got British pounds."

"Never mind."

"Next time I will pay you double. Cheers for now."

Megan was sitting in the kitchen, enjoying a cup of tea when Dai entered.

"Hi honey, I'm home!"

"Don't you 'honey' me David Davies! I don't think what you did was funny!"

Dai tried to play the complete innocent.

"The alarm that you changed! You know I wanted a lie-in today. Now I got one of my heads, thanks to you."

"Sorry, love. Must have been a power cut that caused it. I did not do anything. Anyway I'm off up for a shower. If you want to carry on talking to me, you're more than welcome to join me in the shower."

Megan's expression suggestion that it was highly unlikely he would be enjoying her company.

The water was lovely and hot, reminding Dai of his time down the mines. The thought of a hot shower after work always helped him get through the shift.

Suddenly the hot water turned from hot to freezing, then hot and cold again. Dai shouted downstairs to Megan,

"Are you running the cold water down there? You know it knackers the water up. Will you stop it? I'm in the shower, for goodness sake woman!"

The water then ran just completely cold. Dai switched off the shower. He was colder now than when he was outside standing in the rain. He wrapped the towel around himself, went into the bedroom and found a nice woolly jumper, and jeans. He dressed himself and then went downstairs.

Megan was still sitting there drinking her tea and reading the paper.

"Are you stupid, woman? Why did you run the water when I was in the shower? You know it makes the shower go mental! First it was hot then cold, then back again - and all the time you knew I was in the shower! So, why did you do it?"

"It wasn't me, love. It must have been a power cut that caused it."

The sun finally made an appearance so Dai decided to go for a walk around the village. He always appreciated sunshine after his many years down the mines: 'Unless you worked down there', he would say to people, 'you don't realise how nice it is walking with the sunshine in your face.'

As he passed the Reverend's house he saw Mrs Tompkins with her back towards him, picking up some leaves from around the graves.

"Hello Mrs Tompkins!"

She hadn't realised he was behind her and his voice made her jump.

"My God, Dai! You scared me so much I nearly had forty fits. Are you trying to put me into one of these?" she screamed, pointing to the grave she was tidying. "And if you are, I can't go in this one here, as I don't even know the man."

"Sorry, love. Thought you saw me. Is the Rev in? I fancy a cuppa."

"Well, he's not out here with me, so he must be in there. And if he's not in there or out here, then I don't know where he is. So try in there first as you have already tried here, firstly."

Dai pondered why she had not been admitted to an institution years ago.

"OK, I will try the house."

Dai knocked on the front door.

"Hello, Dai," answered the Reverend. "I saw you talking to Mrs Tompkins, so the kettle's on. Come in."

"I have to ask, Rev," enquired Dai settling back into his chair, "was Mrs Morgan Morgan all right on the way back? She looked a bit peaky as she was leaving."

"Well, I was the last one to be dropped off and she said to me that she would not be out and about today as she had a migraine coming on. She was going to have a quiet day in the house. You know she suffers from migraines, so I don't think there is anything to concern yourself with."

The Reverend drank some of his tea then resumed conversation.

"I think I was right yesterday when we were in the pub and I said that you had a soft spot for her. I think she's grown on you in the last month or so. But it's OK, there's nothing to be ashamed of deep down: I know she is a real nice person."

Dai nearly choked on his tea.

"What you mean? She's grown on me? Weeds grow out in the beer garden and they are not nice. Deep down I was only asking, as a fellow member of the government. The thing is, we were all soaked to the skin this morning and she is so old she remembers the Dead Sea when it wasn't dead but was only ill."

"So, you are concerned for the old people then, are you? And is that the reason why you came down to see me?"

"Yes, being the youngest member of our government I have decided to check on the older members of the cabinet."

"You're only ten years younger than me, David Davies. So you're no spring chicken yourself. I could run rings around you even though I'm older than you. Also, I'm as ripe as rain so there's no need to concern yourself. Anyway, to calm your fears I will pop over to see Mrs Morgan Morgan later, just to make sure she is OK. Then I will pop up to the pub to see you as I think I might need a rum later to warm the old bones: I don't want to come down with a chill at my age. Maybe you should join me as we both know that 'cold kills the old', so it's better to be safe than sorry."

"In that case, I better go and check if I got enough rum for the both of us, and if I don't I will ask P.C. Williams to put his undertakers clothes on and fetch his tape measure with him, to make sure he gets our measurements right! Thanks for the cuppa, I will see myself out. See you tonight. Stay warm."

Dai was later sitting in the *Drag and Daff* telling a couple of the locals about the fun they had that morning at the expense of Mr Fresty, when the phone rang.

"Hang on. I will be right back. You got to hear the end of it."

He hurried to the bar's phone.

"*Drag and Daff.* Dai speaking."

"Hello Dai," replied the Reverend. "Listen boyo: I got something important to ask you."

"Sorry, Rev. We don't do deliveries. If you want a rum you're going to have to come up here for it!"

"No Dai. This is important."

"What's wrong?"

"Well, I went over to Mrs Morgan Morgan's house earlier to check on her. Luckily I met Mrs Tompkins on the way as she cleans for Mrs Morgan Morgan twice a week. I didn't know she cleaned for her until today but anyway we both went in and found Mrs Morgan Morgan collapsed on the floor, unconscious. So we phoned for an ambulance and she has been rushed to hospital. They asked Mrs Tompkins to go with her, as she is a female."

For the first time Dai actually felt a touch guilty.

"How can I help? Tell me. I will do it: no problem."

"Well, would it be possible if you could drive me to the hospital? I would like to be there for her when she wakes up."

"No problem. Give me ten minutes and I will be with you."

He then went to look for Megan, calling loudly for her.

"What's with all the shouting, Dai? You know I got one of my heads."

"Well change it for a different head. I got to go to the hospital with the Reverend. Mrs Morgan Morgan's been rushed in."

"What's she been rushed in with, Dai?" she asked him trying to calm him down.

"I don't know. I'm not a doctor, am I? I got to pick the Reverend up as we need to get over there straight away. I will ring you when I know anything, so you will need to look after the pub. Can you do that, then? Sorry... of course you can. I will ring you when I can."

Dai grabbed the car keys off the hook and rushed out through the door. Twenty minutes later the Reverend and Dai were on the road to Brynlog heading towards its general hospital. They did not say much to each other on the way but both hoped that when they arrived, Mrs Morgan Morgan would be sitting up in bed giving orders left, right and centre to all the poor doctors and nurses within earshot.

Dai pulled into the first available parking space. They then both walked as fast as they could to the information desk just by the entrance.

"How's Mrs Morgan Morgan, please?" Dai asked of the girl sitting behind the desk.

"I'm sorry, I don't know who you mean."

"Excuse me, young lady," intervened the Reverend. "A Mrs Morgan Morgan was rushed here earlier by ambulance. Could you please tell me where we can find her if possible?"

"One moment, please."
She picked up the telephone to make enquiries.

"She has been moved from Accident and Emergency and is now on Primrose Ward. It's the last ward on the left."

Dai and the Reverend headed off to find the room. They passed seven wards en route, all named after flowers: Bluebell, Hyacinth and so on until they reached Primrose. Dai opened the outer doors and both headed towards the nurse's desk.

"Hello," smiled the Reverend. "Could you tell me what bed Mrs Morgan Morgan is in, please? We wish to visit her."

"I'm sorry. At the moment she cannot receive any visitors as the doctors are with her. Please take a seat in the day room, and as soon as you can see her I will call you."

Dai and the Reverend complied. Mrs Tompkins was already sitting there. She looked up at the two of them.

"Oh no! She's dead!"

"Well, the nurse just told us that the doctors were with her, so we thought she was still alive. When did she pass?" asked the Reverend gently.

"I don't know. She was alive when I left."

"Hang on," interjected Dai. "I'm confused. Who told you she had died?"

"Nobody did."

"Well, how the hell do you know she's dead, then?"

Mrs Tompkins looked back up at the pair of them, still shaking her head.

"Well, the Reverend's here so she must be. You are here to comfort us, aren't you Reverend?"

Dai was now also shaking his head but not in sorrow.

"You stupid female! The Reverend is here, like you and me, to visit her - not to give her the last rites!"

"Well, you could have said that beforehand and not let me think she was dead!"

"You didn't give us a chance."

"Oh sit down and relax you two," ordered the Reverend. "This is not going to help anyone, is it? Look, I will go and see if I can get us all a cup of tea to calm our nerves."

"I'm sorry I shouted at you, Mrs Tompkins. It's just been a bit of a stressful day, that's all."

"You should try and keep calm. It's no good getting stressed. If you want a bit of advice, you should try some cauliflower tea. I drink it every morning and you never see me stressed. I am also always as sharp as a tack."

The Reverend returned with three cups of tea on a tray.

"That was really nice of her," he commented of the nurse. "I mean, I asked her to direct me to the tea-vending machine and instead she told me to wait there and she would make us a tea instead. It's nice to have a helpful person now and again."

"Most probably trying to get on your good side. Maybe she's a sinner like me. With all the deaths in hospital, maybe she's hedging her bets?"

"Well Dai, she still stands a chance - unlike you: it's the hot place for you!"

"You going somewhere hot on holidays, then, you and Megan like? I heard Spain is quite hot. Are you going there?" enquired Mrs Tompkins.

"So, this cauliflower tea you drink…it's good for the brain as well, is it?"

"Oh yes," Mrs Tompkins replied.

"Well I think I will stick to alcohol instead: more fun and more tasty!"

"You say you drink cauliflower tea," queried the Reverend of her. "Are you sure about that?"

"I can assure you that I do. I should know: I'm the one who drinks it."

"Well, I have never heard of cauliflower tea. How do you make it?"

"Oh, I don't make it. I buy it when I go to Brynlog market: it's already in teabags - it's with the other fruit-flavoured ones."

"Shouldn't it be in the vegetable department? I will definitely have to look out for it next time I'm in Brynlog - or behind enemy lines, as it is now called."

"I did buy some fruit-flavoured ones a few months back," announced Dai. "Megan had seen this advert on television and it was supposed to give you energy and one of your five-a-day. Well, the way Megan drinks tea it was more like your five-an-hour, not a day. I think I bought elderflower tea. It was not to my taste but Megan liked it."

"That's it! Elderflower. That's what I buy. Sorry! I always get those two mixed up!"

"Well, in that case I won't come around for Sunday dinner. I don't think elderflower would go well with Yorkshire pudding and gravy!"

"Who has that for Sunday dinner, then Dai?"

"Who has what?"

"Elderflower with Yorkshire pudding and gravy? You don't have it, do you? That sounds a bit weird. But if you like it, then it's your choice."

Dai turned to the Reverend.

"When's the next plane to Spain, Rev? It's got to be better than here!"

They sat there chatting for a while before a nurse entered the room.

"You are able to visit Mrs Morgan Morgan now but she is very tired. So please don't stay too long."

"May I ask," enquired the Reverend getting to his feet, "have you found out what's wrong with her?"

"I'm sorry. You will have to ask the doctor in charge for more details. But I did hear them say it might be either a really bad chest infection or even a slight heart attack. I can't tell you anymore than that I'm afraid."

The nurse led them into a side room where Mrs Morgan Morgan was propped upon two pillows. An intravenous drip and heart monitor were also attached to her. Mrs Morgan Morgan opened her eyes as they entered.

"Hello, how are you feeling?" asked the Reverend. "You gave us quite a nasty shock earlier when we found you on the floor."

"When was I on the floor? I don't remember that! Are you sure it was not someone else?"

"No, I found you in your hallway," asserted Mrs Tompkins. "We thought you were dead, or even worse than that."

"What could be worse than 'dead'? Dai asked.

"Well, she might have been in the bath when she collapsed. That would be worse. Imagine being found in the nuddy. If I was not dead before that I would die of embarrassment, let me tell you!"

"Well, the doctors think you either have a bad chest infection or you have had a slight heart attack but it's too early to say. But at least you're still alive, that's the main thing," smiled the Reverend.

"Sorry to disappoint you, David the Public House, but you can't get rid of me that easily."

"That's a horrible thing to say! I will have you know that Dai was very concerned about you. As soon as I told him what was going on, he picked me up and we rushed over here. He was actually very concerned about you!"

"Well, in that case please accept my apology. It must be the tablets they have given me. I'm not normally this nasty - must be the side-effects."

"You must have been on them a long time then! Since I known you, in fact."

"Well, that did not last long, did it? Your concern, that is. You come here and have a go at me. I'm not a well woman. I could be at death's door for all you know."

"You want me to open it for you? Oh sorry, I must be on the same tablets as you!"

Mrs Morgan Morgan closed her eyes. All of a sudden the alarm on the heart monitor rang: the heart trace had flat-lined. The nurse came running in.

"Oh no, not again!" she sighed, and hit the top of the machine. The trace resumed.

"Sorry about that. It's a dodgy connection. We are waiting for another one to be bought up to us from another ward."

Mrs Tompkins was shaking in fright.

"For a moment then I thought she was dead!"

"Charming! I only wanted to rest my eyes for five minutes and you were ready to sort out the sandwiches for my wake!"

"She will be all right, honest! She can't die as God doesn't want her and the Devil is scared in case she takes over."

The nurse returned.

"I'm sorry but I'm going to have to ask you all to leave now as Matron Morgan Morgan is very tired and needs to rest. You can come back tomorrow afternoon. Visiting time is between 2.30 and 4pm.

The Reverend and Mrs Tompkins wished their patient farewell but before Dai left, he walked up to Mrs Morgan Morgan and kissed her gently on the forehead.

"Get well soon you old battle-axe!" he whispered. "Otherwise I won't have anyone to fight with if you snuff it."

Dai left her bedside and approached the nurse who had just spoken to them.

"I have to ask, just now you said 'Matron' Morgan Morgan, not 'Mrs'. How did you know she used to be a matron?"

"She has told us more than once since she arrived here. And when you're on your way out, just have a look outside Daffodil Ward. You will see an old photo taken in the 1950s. See if you can spot her? She had to tell me which one it was: I would never have guessed in a million years!"

They all headed down the main corridor and stopped when they arrived at Daffodil.

"See if either of you can tell me which one she is, then? challenged the Reverend. "I already know as I have been a regular visitor here at the hospital for the past ten years."

"Were they sick before you visited them or only after?"

Mrs Tompkins looked hard at the photo.

"I got it!" she exclaimed "but I'm not telling you. Dai, see if you can spot her?"

Dai scanned the photograph slowly.

"Nope. I can't spot her. Which one is it?"

"There she is," beamed Mrs Tompkins proudly.

The Reverend laughed.

"That's not her! That is Doctor Trevor Williams."

"Is it her brother?" Mrs Tompkins asked, "as they do look alike."

"I now give up twice," declard Dai. "First, on this one," pointing at the photo, "and definitely on this one," he said, pointing at Mrs Tompkins.

The Reverend pointed at a very young attractive nurse.

"There she is!"

"Are you pulling my leg? That's never her! She's too pretty and young. She's nothing like that old battle-axe we just visited."

"I was the same as you when I first saw it I must admit," laughed the Reverend. "I was a bit shocked as well."

"Well, no wonder three men married her. Pity she killed them all off, though."

Mrs Tompkins smacked Dai's arm.

"You can't say that out loud. You never know who might be listening. You don't want to get her into trouble and get her sent to prison, do you?"

Dai briefly pondered the vision of Mrs Morgan Morgan in court, sentenced to life without parole, and then smiled.

"Come back to us, Dai!" laughed the Reverend. "Did you just imagine Mrs Morgan Morgan going to prison for murder?"

"Of course not! I wasn't imagining her in court for murder at all. It was mass murder actually!"

Mrs Tompkins slapped him once more.

When Dai returned to the *Drag and Daff* he saw that the bar was full of locals. Megan hushed the crowd.

"Well, Dai? How is Mrs Morgan Morgan? What did they say was wrong with her?"

Dai recounted the information they had received. Paula the Post then approached him him with a pot full of notes and coins.

"We heard what happened and have had a whip-round to buy her some flowers. There's over 100 Glas here! We were not sure how bad she was, so did not know whether to buy a bouquet or a wreath. So, here's the money instead. You can get her a nice bouquet of flowers tomorrow."

Megan took the money off Dai.

"I think it would be better if I got the flowers knowing the way you two fight. You would end up buying her a wreath of deadly nightshade and poison ivy!"

Dai just poured himself a pint.

"Ladies and gentlemen," he boomed. "Ladies and gentlemen. I would like to propose a toast: to Mrs Morgan Morgan. Get well soon…and to all of you: we may be a New

Aberglas in a New Wales but we still have old-fashioned values and care."

A week later Mrs Morgan Morgan was discharged. The Reverend had taken her to the *Dragon and Daffodil* for one of Megan's famous Sunday roasts. Despite Dai's protests it was 'on the house' and as usual, the pub was packed even though it was only non-alcoholic drinks that could be served on that day. The locals looked forward to Sunday lunch regardless as people always said "a Sunday roast for a fiver? You can't cook it for less and you don't have to do the washing up afterwards! Tidy, that is". Megan had bought a beautiful bouquet of flowers and presented it to Mrs Morgan Morgan after she had finished her meal. For the first time in ages Mrs Morgan Morgan smiled without saying something sarcastic first.

Dai walked over to her as Megan presented the bouquet.

"Don't you dare try and kiss me again David the Public House! It took me three baths to get rid of the smell of you from the last time you kissed me!"

The doctors finally discovered the cause of Mrs Morgan Morgan's malady: she had indeed contracted a serious chest infection partly attributable to standing outside in the rain at the protest and partly because she was not using the central heating she had had installed in her cottage. She had argued with the doctors, claiming that during the war they never had central heating and neither the Nazis nor the cold weather had killed her then. The doctors tried to explain that she was not as young as she used to be and that if she was ever admitted into hospital again with a chest infection due to lack of heat in her cottage, they would recommend that she was put in a sheltered housing complex. This genuinely terrified her but she kept it to herself.

Dai had been running a bet in the pub over what he thought was wrong with Mrs Morgan Morgan, with all proceeds going towards the chapel's roof fund. It was 1 Glas a go and the winner would get a free pint of bitter - or a small glass of wine. The top three diagnoses were: foot and mouth; swine flu and mad cow disease. Mrs Morgan Morgan actually picked out the winner from the hat, and the winning diagnosis was: mad cow disease. Colin the Cabbie was the actual victor, and then had to apologise to Mrs Morgan Morgan. To make amends he bought her a double vodka and coke, which actually cost him 3 Glas and 60 Abers. If he had not won, it would have only cost him 1 Glas and 95 Abers for a pint of bitter but he was still happy: "I never normally have any luck in raffles!" Dai wondered if he was related to Mrs Tompkins.

Dai returned to the bar and rang the bell to call for order: he had an important letter to read out. The entire pub fell silent.

"To the new government of New Aberglas New Wales, still no postcode yet.

To whom it may concern,
I write to you on behalf of the British government in London to confirm receipt of a completed document from the Welsh government in Cardiff regarding your intention to become independent.

This is the first occasion we have ever had to deal with such a request which we believe arose from the possibility of your village being twinned with another in Europe.

We fully intended to oppose this but being contacted by a colleague of one Mr Fresty, we learnt what had subsequently taken place and iimmediately withdrew our objections. We were informed that after you held a meeting with Mr Fresty at your new government building, he did not achieve the outcome he desired so took it upon himself to force his way into your village, accompanied by two members of the police force and his own personal solicitor.

We, unreservedly, would like to apologise for his actions. It had been our intention to invite him to a disciplinary hearing but unfortunately before this could be arranged we learnt that he had been sectioned under the Mental Health Act. This apparently occurred after police were called to his office following reports of his being dressed in ladies' clothes and shouting, 'I will show them who's transparent' at the top of his voice.

We would therefore like to welcome you to Wales and the United Kingdom, and if there is anything we can ever do to assist you in the future, please do not hesite to make contact with us again.
Yours faithfully,
Michael Stone,

Member of Parliament.

The whole pub stood up and started to cheer. Dai called the Reverend and Mrs Morgan Morgan over to join him, which caused the crowd to clap even harder. The Reverend waited patiently for the crowd to hush before addressing them.

"My fellow Aberglassens. It is with immense pride that we have beaten the big boyos at last. They may have regarded us as a little puppy trying to make a big noise but they now realise that in fact we are a roaring, fire-breathing dragon. Now, the first thing we must decide as a new country is which country to twin with? But before you give us your suggestions, I have heard of a little country called Wales which sounds very nice - but it's up to you!"

"You can choose any country you wish," declared Mrs Morgan Morgan getting to her feet, "but anyone who does not choose Wales will be thrown out of this country and never allowed to return! So, if you ever fancy visiting Llancoch Castle one day, why not stop off and visit a different country on the way? You're welcome, as long as you have your passport with you, and Paula the Post does a very good exchange rate on Abers and Glas - and you will always get a warm welcome at the *Dragon and Daffodil* public house. And, as it says above the bar door: 'We may not be part of old Wales anymore but we can still cwtch'."

Printed in Great Britain
by Amazon